The
GOLDEN KEY
of
GANGOTRI

The
GOLDEN KEY
of
GANGOTRI

EYAL N. DANON

To my children,
Maya, Jonathan and Daniel

"Our deepest fears are like dragons
guarding our deepest treasure."

— Rainer Maria Rilke

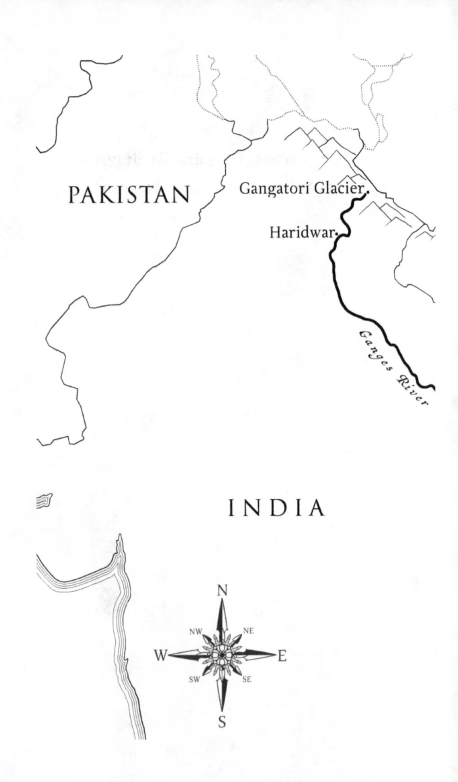

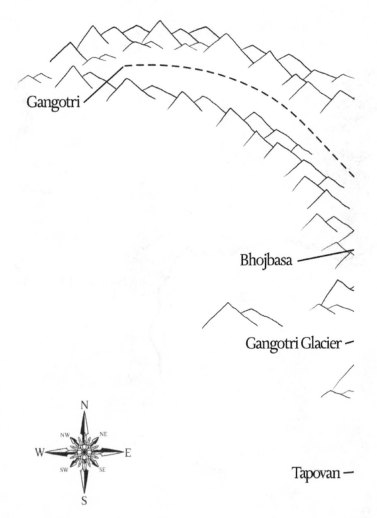

Gangotri

Bhojbasa —

Gangotri Glacier —

Tapovan —

N
NW NE
W — E
SW SE
S

CHAPTER 1

HARLEY FELT A TAP ON her shoulder and opened her eyes. The passenger sitting beside her had woken her up. The sun piercing through the bus window colored him gold. Raising his arm, he pointed at the surrounding view. "Rishikesh," he said and looked out the window. Harley stretched, and as she ran her fingers through her tangled hair, they grazed the painful bruise on her forehead. She bit her lip and looked around. On her left, green mountains sloped down gently toward the road. In the opposite direction she saw the Ganges River and a string of white-and-pink temples on the riverbank. The tips of other temples, hidden deep inside the green mountains, glowed in the distance. She recalled this was the very place where the Ganges completed its long journey from the Himalayas and began winding its way throughout India, and her heart swelled.

The pilgrims filed off the bus and headed straight to the river, speaking to each other in brisk sentences. Harley followed them. They passed through an area on the riverbank that was flat and full of small white rocks. Huge purple rhododendrons flowers surrounded them, and the blue-green water flowed quickly down the wide river. When the pilgrims arrived at the edge of the water, they wasted no time before going in, fully clothed. Faces aglow, they rejoiced at having made it to the mouth of the Ganges.

Harley observed them for a few minutes, then took off her shoes and placed them near her backpack. She removed her wristwatch, shoving it deep inside her bag, and walked into the river, still wearing her clothes. The frozen water was rejuvenating. Dunking her whole head in, she felt all the aches from the night ride evaporate and her thoughts become clear and sharp. She carried a silent prayer of gratitude for having made it, for being alive and breathing and experiencing life with such clarity. She had no idea how the adventure she had gotten herself into might end, but was finally living the life she had always wanted to live, freely and bravely. She smiled, and the Indians nearby smiled back, happy to see this Western tourist connecting to the ancient ritual of bathing in the holy river.

After the refreshing dip, the pilgrims sat down and drank sweet hot chai. Harley held the steaming cup and felt a strange camaraderie with the group gathered on the banks of the sacred river. She began walking toward the main road. Rishikesh was bustling and noisy. Buses and trucks passed through with loud honks; peddlers hawked their wares with hoarse shouts; and rickshaw drivers artfully navigated the chaos. This was a far cry from the quiet, peaceful town Harley had envisioned. A rickshaw driver pulled up and signaled her with his weathered hand. She gave him the name of the ashram and he nodded, then loaded her backpack at the rear of the rickshaw. Harley sat in the back and he sped off, honking a loud horn every chance he got.

Within ten minutes they arrived at their destination. Harley descended from the rickshaw near a magnificent metal bridge that crossed the river and walked closer so she could examine its beauty. She had long admired beautiful structures and had spent countless hours drawing bridges of every kind. *Once I cross this bridge*, she thought, *I can no longer go back.* Engrossed in the moment, she had failed to notice the fading noise of the rickshaw's engine. She turned her head and saw the rickshaw in the distance, disappearing around the bend. Harley began running toward the bend in the road. There she saw a bustling main street crammed with trucks and buses, all creating a commotion. The rickshaw driver and her backpack were nowhere to be seen. A peddler approached her proffering packs of chewing gum. With a wave of her hand, she sent him away and scoured the street for a police officer. Soon she gave up, overtaken by a sickening feeling. The driver had no intention of coming back. She had just lost all the possessions she had brought with her for the journey, and one possession that was more important than all the others combined.

Harley's father's letter was lost forever. It had never occurred to her to make a copy. She naively assumed that his letter was going to accompany her for the rest of her life. Her eyes welled up. Sitting by the side of the road, she covered her face with her hands. *This should not have happened to me*, she said to herself over and over again. *This should not have happened!* After some time had passed, she raised her head. A few small children were curiously staring at her but did not dare approach. She wished so badly for some miracle that would make the driver suddenly return but knew he would not.

Harley peered up at the bridge. She had to continue her journey but lacked the strength to move. A small monkey was curiously looking at her, hanging on a tree branch. When she saw the monkey, she instinctively touched the pouch that her mother had given her back in New York. Taking a deep breath, she turned toward the flowing river. After a while she felt her body begin to calm. The current crashed against the smooth white rocks and her thoughts wandered to a time a few months back, to that fateful morning at faraway Columbia University in New York. She was a student at the college, where, during a morning class about sacred landmarks in India, a single word was destined to change her fate forever.

At the word *Gangotri*, Harley sat up straight. Something had awakened within her, urging her to focus on what was being said. She surveyed her classmates. No one reacted as she had. She tried to conceal her sudden excitement and looked out the large old windows at the pouring rain. A refreshing breeze gusted through the window screens as Dr. Mark Shelby, a world-renowned professor of Eastern cultures, described pilgrimage sites located in a remote and wild part of the Indian Himalayas. He was a tall dark-haired man in his early fifties with an athletic build. He moved nimbly across the large classroom and paused his lecture to pick up a piece of paper from the floor. He turned the paper over and when he saw that it was filled with scribbles and doodles, he crumpled it into a ball and threw it with a long circular motion toward a green bin in the corner. The ball hit the rim and went in. Behind Harley, someone clapped. Professor Shelby smiled, pleased by the applause.

Animatedly, he continued describing how the mighty Ganges, considered to be the world's holiest river, begins in an ice cave at the summit of an isolated glacier on the Tibetan border. From there it flows through the Indian subcontinent until it merges with the Bay of Bengal. Indians believed the sky and earth met precisely at that special place and the devout embarked on their pilgrimage in the freezing cold, lacking appropriate gear. There is a special power to that place, the professor emphasized, and pilgrims believe that arriving at the true source of the holy Ganges River opens the door to understanding ourselves and the world around us.

Someone from the back row called out, "Professor Shelby, did you visit there during one of your adventures?" It was common knowledge that Professor Shelby spent his annual vacation on long adventurous trips across Southeast Asia. A gloomy expression passed over the professor's face before he replied, "There, I have not yet gone."

The question interrupted the flow of Professor Shelby's speech. Staring at an indistinct spot on the wall, he gathered his thoughts and continued his lecture. With his professorial power of observation, he noticed that he had Harley's undivided attention and turned to her enthusiastically. In the student before him he saw a lean girl with an upturned nose, freckles, and piercing green eyes that were concentrating on him. She did not smile. Professor Shelby was now talking about the ancient temple in Gangotri. Harley knew she had heard of that place before, and that it held great significance. Something about that name took her back . . . but to what?

For some reason she could no longer focus. Her father's image appeared in her mind, with his big smile, his arm around an Indian friend, and great snowy mountains in the background. It was the same picture she kept by her bed, the one she spoke to every night before she fell asleep. She thought of the short prayer she used to say before going to bed and began to absentmindedly doodle on the piece of paper in front of her. To her surprise, her hand was sketching the mysterious ice cave, surrounded by towering mountains whose peaks brushed the clouds. The cave looked like a dark hole in the middle of the glacier and Harley felt as though she had already been there, that she knew the place. Deep in thought, she added more details to complete the image. Upon hearing her name, she almost jumped out of her chair.

"I hope my class wasn't *that* boring, Ms. Green."

Professor Shelby was standing directly in front of her, staring at her drawing with great interest. The students began leaving the classroom, chattering lively. Harley blushed, folded the paper in half, shoved it in her bag, and turned to the professor.

"I am sorry. For some reason, my mind wandered."

"Sometimes it happens to me during my own lectures," he said, smiling in return.

Harley headed for the door. She had a feeling that Professor Shelby wanted to converse about her drawing, but she was too disoriented to speak coherently. She said goodbye and began walking home.

Harley lived with her mother, Sarah, in an apartment building within walking distance to the university and Central Park. As she walked, she tried remembering where in the world she could had heard about Gangotri, that meeting point of the sky and the earth. Her mind remained blank, but her body felt cold, as if pressed up against a wall of ice. Suddenly Harley lost her balance and fell backward. Without noticing, she had bumped into a sidewalk fruit cart. The neat rows of apples rolled onto the pavement.

"Look what you have done!" a vendor fumed.

"Oh, no, I am sorry," Harley apologized. She bent down and began helping the vendor collect the apples.

Sensing her confusion, the vendor said in a softer tone, "It's alright, no big deal."

She gave him an absentminded smile and offered to buy the apple in her hand. He took it from her, rubbed it on his sleeve, and handed it back. "This one's on me. Just watch where you're going next time."

The apartment was quiet and empty. In the living room, Harley pushed the curtain aside, letting sunlight filter in. At this time of day, her mom was working at her private clinic. Remembering this helped Harley relax for a bit; she wanted to be alone and get to the bottom of the uncanny feeling evoked by that strange name. She turned on the air conditioner, poured herself a bowl of cereal, and sat in front of the picture window overlooking the Hudson River. A few minutes later she got up to wash the dishes. The sensation of the running water helped steady her breath.

She changed into sportswear, grabbed her bike helmet, and went downstairs. Soon she was pedaling toward

Central Park. It was empty at this time of day and she started her usual route around the large lake in the middle of the park. A nice breeze cooled her face. As she rode, she went over what had happened to her that morning. She had a feeling that things were about to change, that her life would no longer be the same, and this left her with mixed emotions. She was excited by the promise change brings, but at the same time she feared the unknown.

Harley opened the bottle of water she had strapped to her bike and drank her fill. When she looked up, she noticed a squirrel on a low branch frozen in place. It then turned its head toward a taller branch close to where it was standing. The squirrel didn't move at all but looked like it was measuring the distance between the branches. Harley continued her route, wondering if the squirrel was ever going to leap.

The flat trail turned into a moderate climb and she switched into a lower gear. On her right she saw a steep slope leading to a clearing in the woods, outside of the marked trail. On previous rides Harley had always passed it by. But this day was different. She felt she was on the cusp of a significant change and spurred herself on to live more daringly, and not become addicted to a false sense of security.

Ever since she was a child, she believed most people chose the safe path in life. She saw herself as an adventurer, taking constant risks to discover new lands. She usually researched the terrain before confronting danger, but this time she simply swerved her bike downward. The wind whistled in her ears as she gripped the handlebars and swerved from side to side, struggling to keep control. She was almost at the end of the slope when her front wheel struck something, spun around, and tilted upward. The handlebars jammed into her ribs and the bike flew from her hands, sending her spiraling into the hard ground. There was no one around. Harley rose slowly, her ribs pierced with pain. She limped toward the bike, picked it up, and headed back for the trail. It was an hour before she made it home.

Back in the apartment, she washed and bandaged her cuts. She took deep, measured breaths to calm down, and soon knew where to look to find the answer to the question that was nagging her. She went into her bedroom and opened the bottom desk drawer. In it was a dreadful mess of notes, erasers, pens, hard candy, hair clips and keys, but she quickly found what she was looking for. Harley pulled out a thin plastic bag with a yellowing envelope inside. The faint postage stamp indicated the letter had been sent from Rishikesh, India. Her pulse quickened as she opened the envelope and removed a piece of paper that was beginning to disintegrate at the margins. Her eyes landed on the top left line, and she smiled. It read "Gangotri, 18 October."

Although she had asked her mother endless questions about what had happened to her father, Sarah was never eager to discuss the matter. As a child Harley would spend hours poring over maps of the Himalayas, tracing with her fingers the paths that, she imagined, led to the spot from which her father had never returned. A strange excitement grabbed hold of her. Clutching the letter, she began reading it.

Harley, my dear daughter!

You have no idea how much I miss you. I think of you when I see all this beauty around me, great snowy mountains with peaks brushing the clouds. At this moment I am looking at the Ganges River flowing over immense white boulders inside a steep canyon. I am among a group of pilgrims that arrived from across India to this sacred place. I have dreamt about this journey for a long time, and here I am now, fulfilling my dream. The feeling is simply wonderful.

I am including in this letter a gift for you—a small golden key. I spent several hours yesterday with an old man as he sat and made jewelry. He made the key from a small piece of gold he melted on the spot. He has been around pilgrimage sites for many years. You would be surprised to hear, but he asked many questions about you, what kind of child you are. He insisted on engraving your name in Sanskrit on the back of the small key. I did not believe he could do it, but as you can see, I too am learning something new every day. Whenever you may need to make an important decision, touch the key, and think about what it is your heart desires.

That is all for now, my beloved daughter. Tomorrow I embark on my adventure in the mountains, so the next letter will arrive after my return.

I love you more than anything in the world!

Dad

When she finished the letter, she grew pensive. She thought about the years that had gone by so quickly. When her father disappeared, she was twelve years old. Eight years had already passed from the time he mysteriously vanished in Indian Himalayas. Time slipped by like a crafty thief that never gets caught. She fingered the golden key pendant around her neck, flipped it over, and marveled at the craftsmanship of the old artist who had managed to engrave her name on such a tiny delicate object. She thought of the sentence her father used to say to her, "Do not fear the fear," and a distant memory resurfaced.

When Harley was ten years old, one beautiful winter day her father had come to her school to pull her out of class. He did not tell her what they were about to do, but by then she was already familiar with his adventurous spirit. Once out of the city, they drove for an hour along the Hudson River. He brought her to a long snowy slope, took a red sled out of the car, and together they began climbing up the mountain. Not a soul was in sight; a yellow sun peered through a blue cloudless sky and the tree branches were covered in thick snow. They left visible tracks in the snow—the giant footprints from her father's large boots next to her own small ones. She marveled at being able to leave such clear tracks in the snow even though she was so little and thought how great it would be if her father's tracks and hers could remain embedded there forever. As far as she was concerned, she would continue walking behind her father until the end of time.

When they arrived at the summit, they looked down. The snowy slope was adorned with bumps and pits. That warm sense of security suddenly evaporated, and a chill traveled down her spine. Her father smiled at her and sat her at the front of the sled, placing himself behind her. Before she could think, they were flying at an incredible speed down the snowy slope. She felt safe with her father at her back, but she still tried to slow the sled with her feet. The wind whistled in their ears, the sled raced forward, and her bursting laughter was equal parts pleasure and horror.

When they went up the mountain again, panting heavily from treading in the heavy snow, her father said to her, "You know, this would be a whole lot more fun if you tucked your feet inside the sled as we go down."

"But Dad, that would be way too fast."

"That's exactly the point," her father said, and his familiar laughter echoed. She glanced at him, shrugged her shoulders, and said, "I don't want to do that."

Sitting on the sled, he invited her to sit near him. He collected fresh snow in the palm of his big hand and let the flakes leisurely fall onto the white bed that surrounded them. Then he looked at Harley and said,

"You can learn to live with your fear and let it make you stronger."

"But how?" she asked.

He smiled at her as his foot nudged the red sled forward. She held her breath and he pushed again, harder than before. She screamed, and he screamed with her, and down they sped, their feet inside the sled, her father holding her, the wind in their eyes and nature all around them. And she knew, with that mysterious sense children have, that this was a moment she would never forget. After several more rounds down the slope, her father took her to a nearby restaurant on the side of the road. Harley asked for hot cocoa with whipped cream and her father raised two fingers to the waitress. Like daughter, like father.

"Don't you want to order something else? Something for grown-ups?" Harley asked in a tone that was almost concerned.

Her father threw his head back and laughed heartily. Then he grew serious, held her small face in both hands, and said, "Sweetheart, remember when you got on the sled and saw the long, scary way down?"

Harley nodded, wide-eyed.

"And how did you feel?"

She hesitated. "Happy—no, scared—no, happy and scared at the same time, I think."

Harley's father smiled and nodded.

"You know," he said, "there's an old Native American saying: 'Leap into the abyss and the net will appear.'"

Harley pouted her lips as she drank the hot cocoa. "But what if I leap and discover there is no net down there?"

"That's also a possibility," her father admitted.

"That doesn't sound like such a good deal to me; leaping into a scary abyss only to crash at the bottom with no safety net."

He looked at her, his eyes shining mischievously. He leaned forward from his chair and said, "We have to jump into the abyss because the key to your freedom is at the bottom."

Harley furrowed her brow toward the bridge of her small, upturned nose and asked, "Which key? What does it open?"

"This key, if you can find it, will bring you the biggest gift life can provide—freedom from all of your fears. It will also show you how to be happy, regardless of what other people think of you."

"I don't know, leaping into the unknown sounds too dangerous."

"It is not an actual abyss," he smiled again and tousled his daughter's hair. "And it gets easier with each leap. In time you will understand what I am talking about."

Harley looked at her father's handwriting and tears began to fill her eyes. She missed his embrace and his sense of humor, his rare ability to downplay every crisis and render it insignificant. After her father disappeared, she found no one else she could talk to about anything beyond the everyday existence everyone around her was so busy with. But she never ceased to feel there was something beyond this ordinary life, something marvelous revealed only to those who knew where to look. She enrolled as an architecture major at Columbia University, and for her minor she chose East Asian studies. That's how she ended up in Professor Shelby's class on holy pilgrimage sites in India. But to her disappointment, all the books and classes she took only deepened her confusion and flooded her mind with a torrent of conflicting ideas and words. She knew she had to search for this secret knowledge out in the world, but until now she had no clear idea where to start. Taking stock of the things those around her held dear, she was astounded that people could waste their lives chasing after comfort, security, and superficial pleasures without attempting to understand life's true meaning.

Her mother dedicated all her time to her but was unable to answer Harley's complex questions. Harley understood long ago that her mother was a practical woman who had raised her with a mixture of deep love and an expectation of excellence, a mother who pushed her forward whenever Harley needed encouragement or a receptive ear. Even though Sarah worked as a psychologist with a demanding schedule, she knew how to juggle her work and caring for her only child. It was only recently that Harley noticed her mother had stopped buying new clothes and going out in the evenings. Sarah's life revolved around her daughter and her work. She did not try to meet new men and rarely participated in social gatherings.

Harley returned to thinking about her father's mysterious disappearance in the Himalayas and about the magical place described by Professor Shelby, the location from which her father sent his final letter. She felt a strange pull to that enigmatic place—Gangotri. For the first time she could understand what had compelled her father to go there. Professor Shelby's description left no room for doubt. The fact that Gangotri drew believers who, for hundreds of years, had been arriving by every means from across India to bathe at the source of the world's holiest river, was proof positive that this place left its mark on every visitor. She thought of her father, and how she could better understand what had happened to him. Her mother still refused to discuss it. She dismissed Harley's questions by repeating, "He disappeared in the

Himalayas; there is nothing more to say." Now, although she could not explain it, Harley sensed that her father's disappearance had to do with Gangotri. Her heart told her so.

She approached the bookcase and pulled out an old photo album containing photographs of her father and mother during their trip to India, while they were in college. Seeing the two of them, both with long hair, wearing flowing white shirts and striped red-and-blue bell-bottom pants, still made her laugh. In the photos they looked happy and young against the backdrop of bustling cities and green mountains.

Harley sat on the armchair and adjusted her position to relieve some of the pain in her ribs. She was exhausted, both inside and out. From where she sat, a picture of a massive wave at the heart of the ocean peered back at her from the opposite wall. It was by a Japanese artist whose name Harley could never remember. The wave appeared to be in the middle of nowhere, just a perfect force of nature at the heart of a vast ocean, where no observer could ever witness it. It seemed to Harley that this picture had been with her for her entire life. Whenever she looked at it, she envisioned herself surfing that giant wave until she safely reached the shore. Harley opened her eyes wider; she stared at the image until a sweet fatigue spread through her limbs.

CHAPTER 2

HARLEY WAS CLIMBING THE GLACIER in the Himalayas—the one leading to the ice cave—to the source of the Ganges River. She was panting and stopped to look at the stars lighting the sky, the color of which fluctuated between black and deep blue. The mighty mountain peaks surrounded her. There was not a thing in sight but the full moon coloring everything a hypnotic white. A voice inside told her she should backtrack, forget this quest, and stop before she made it to the ice cave. She ignored the alarm bells ringing in her ears and kept climbing, one step at a time, sinking her feet in the heavy snow. Ahead of her she saw the last incline before the top of the glacier and sighed in relief. Right then strong winds came out of nowhere, threatening to blow her deep into the abyss. She walked against the direction of the strong wind howling in her ears and pulled herself up with difficulty, her muscles straining. Though the exertion racked her entire body, she knew that she couldn't stop now, so close to her destination.

At last, she reached the top and rested on the flat ice. The wind stopped blowing. The moon appeared within reach and cast an eerie light all around. At the edge of the ice plane, she saw a lofty wall of ice. Translucent channels ran up and down it as it released water into a frozen pool from a deep and dark opening at the wall's base. She noticed the shadow of a figure sitting near the cave entrance and her heart skipped a beat.

The voice inside warned her again, urging her to go back and not approach the sitting figure. She ignored it and began walking toward the cave, dumbfounded when she realized her steps did not leave any tracks in the snow.

The figure was wrapped in an orange cape. His legs were crossed. A voice whispered to her: *See, this is your father, he is right here.* This is the moment she had dreamt about so many times. Her quest was finally over. She laughed out loud, waved her hands, and yelled out his name. But the figure didn't turn, and her own voice sounded strange to her, as if it were disappearing down an endless tunnel. Harley ran forward expectantly, slipping and scratching her arms on the boulders guarding the cave. When she reached the cave's entrance, the figure slowly turned to face her. She held her breath but before she could see his face, she woke up, gasping for air.

Harley inhaled and tried to steady her breathing. Pans were clanging in the kitchen, and the smell of fresh coffee penetrated her nostrils. She again reminded herself that after all these years, there was no chance that her father was still alive. And yet the dream filled her with excitement. Opening her eyes, she sat up on the sofa, turned toward the kitchen, and saw that her mom was making pancakes, whistling a jovial tune to herself, moving swiftly from pan to pan. Harley studied her mother's slim figure and long wavy hair.

"You slept well, I hope," Sarah said with a big smile when she noticed her daughter looking at her.

"Yeah, I dozed off," Harley said. "I had such a strange dream. It felt so real."

"And what's the mysterious treasure you were after this time? Which faraway country were you exploring?"

Harley laughed. It was their own private joke. Ever since she was a child Harley wondered what she was destined to do with her life. She always loved to draw and was attracted to designing beautiful buildings and bridges, and for a while she thought that studying architecture in college would calm her down. But it didn't. The sense that there was something marvelous beyond ordinary life and everyday reality continued to haunt her. She didn't know exactly what to look for but had a clear sense that to find out what was the meaning of her life, she needed to live an unconventional life, one that was shared by the few, not the many.

This realization made her marvel at the fact that the people in her life did not see the world the same way she did. She asked her mother about far-flung relatives, trying to find someone in her family who lived off the beaten path. Her mother answered her questions patiently, but Harley felt there was another dimension to life, beyond the obvious and mundane, that her mother could not access. Sarah called on her from the small kitchen,

"How about some hot pancakes with blueberries and whipped cream?"

"Come on, Mom. Who could say no to that?" Harley stretched, and grimaced in pain.

"What's wrong?" Sarah asked.

"I'm fine. I just went down a steep slope in a reckless manner."

"Let me look at you," Sarah demanded. She examined the deep elbow gash and shook her head. After she cleaned and disinfected the cuts, she moved on to the bruised ribs. It hurt like hell, but Harley did not make a sound.

Sarah looked at Harley and frowned. "Alarm bells must have gone off in your head before you decided to go down that slope. What made you do something so dangerous?"

"I thought I could do it," Harley said.

"Well, I don't know how many times you need to learn that every mistake you make comes with a price," Sarah said and pointed her chin toward the dining room table. "Let's eat before the pancakes get cold."

"Let's!" Harley said and sat down to eat with her mother.

"And how was your day going before you fell?" Sarah asked.

"There was a fascinating lecture at the university," Harley replied, happy to change the subject. "This is the elective course that I'm taking with Professor Shelby.

Today he talked about pilgrimage sites in India, and the amazing efforts of pilgrims trying to reach remote places in the Himalayas."

At the mention of Professor Shelby's name, her mother's facial expression changed. Harley knew the two had studied together at the same university years before, and for some reason had failed to keep in touch. In fact, the only time they'd encountered each other, during a reception for new students, her mother had been rigid and tense, and Professor Shelby himself seemed withdrawn. As they exchanged a few pleasantries, Harley could not help but note their visible discomfort. She later asked her mother if she had known Professor Shelby well when they were students. Her mother shook her head and said that he was a bright and lonely student who did not try to befriend others.

Harley poured piping hot coffee into her mother's mug. "And how was your day?"

"Actually, I've had a rough day," her mom sighed as she stacked the hot pancakes onto her daughter's plate. She looked up from the table and Harley could see the tiredness in her blue eyes.

"One of my patients is simply not showing any progress," her mother said and shook her head. She added a dollop of whipped cream to the pancakes, sprinkled nuts on top, and decorated the plate with juicy blueberries.

"What are you working on?"

Harley's mom exhaled in frustration and said, "It's a young man who says his dream is to become a professional guitarist. But he's not spending enough time practicing or auditioning. He tried to audition for local bands a number of times, but they've all told him he isn't ready."

"So why doesn't he just practice more?" Harley asked.

"I think he's afraid of what he'll discover once he really gives the guitar his all. What would happen then, after all that practice and effort? What will he do if he learns that his dream isn't achievable?"

"And how do you see his future?" Harley furrowed her brow.

"He's already spent ten years of his life pursuing his dream of becoming a professional guitarist. But he didn't do it the right way. He should have invested a massive effort from the get-go. He should have pursued his dream as if his life depended on it."

"I see," Harley said, surprised at the dramatic way her mother described the situation.

Sarah looked at her daughter and then turned her gaze toward the picture of the wave hanging on the wall across from them. She pointed at it with her left hand.

"Imagine if you tried hanging a frameless picture on your wall. The picture would begin to fold at the edges, and after some time it would lose all its beauty. Now consider a nicely framed picture, sealed and taut at the edges. If you were to hang that picture, you could enjoy its beauty for years. People are like that as well. To develop properly we need a strong frame that can provide the inner tension we need to reach our goals."

Harley considered her mother's words. Something about the metaphor bothered her. "And what if the picture frame doesn't fit? What if the frame is just too tight?"

"You don't stay frozen in time inside one picture. Life is dynamic, and the secret is to figure out when to move on, to try something new."

"When to move on . . ." Harley said, repeating her mother's words, trying to understand them.

"Yes, look at you," said Sarah. "You are almost done with your architecture studies, and you have already applied to the graduate architecture program at Columbia. You're doing the right thing by moving from one challenge to the next but focusing your energy in the same area."

Harley nodded and said nothing. Her mother had pushed her to apply to the prestigious graduate program, but Harley wasn't sure she wanted to dedicate several more years to academic studies. Sarah looked at her daughter for a long moment, smiled, and said, "Speaking of moving on, are these pancakes cheering you up?"

Harley smiled with her mouth full and continued stuffing her face, piling on a second helping of whipped cream. She drank the strong hot coffee and when she looked up, she saw her mother regarding her with incredible affection. *It's so good I have someone who loves me so much*, she thought. Harley knew her mother would do anything for her and knowing this filled her with gratitude laced with anxiety. She was anxious about the inevitable moment in which she would be forced to disappoint her mother in one way or another. Harley knew the day would come when she would have to make her own way in the world, and there was a distinct possibility her choices would not measure up to what her mother had in mind for her.

As Harley placed the dishes in the sink and watched the faucet's water flow, she remembered the source of the Ganges, the ice cave in her dream, Gangotri. She realized the possibility that her choices would not measure up to what her mother had in mind for her were now more distinct than ever before. She kept this thought to herself.

Maybe her mother was right. Perhaps one needed to work within the boundaries of a tight framework, trying to figure out what life was all about. Harley wanted to believe her mother, but something powerful inside her was stirring up—a quiet determination to make her own decisions, pushing her to take a leap of faith into the unknown.

CHAPTER 3

HARLEY DIDN'T FEEL SHE COULD confide in her
mother about wanting to follow in her father's footsteps.
She knew that Sarah had traveled to India in the past, but
she feared her reaction. Her mother would probably try
to persuade her to stay put, and within her sights. Harley
wanted to speak with someone who knew India well, but
not about what had happened to her father. There was
only one person who came to mind—her professor, Dr.
Mark Shelby.

When she arrived at his office at Columbia, she noticed
a sign which read No Office Hours on Wednesdays. It was
Wednesday. She knocked on the door.

"Who is it?" a slightly hoarse voice sounded from
inside the office.

Without replying, she turned the doorknob and opened
the door. If this brazenness caught Professor Shelby off
guard, you couldn't see it on his face. He was writing in
a journal bound in leather. A half-eaten piece of apple pie
was on his desk, and through the big window behind him
she could see a red cherry tree. Professor Shelby looked
inquisitively at the girl. Harley walked to the center of

the room and stood in front of his desk. She knew the professor's pleasant demeanor could change in an instant if he felt his time was being wasted. She gathered herself and said, "I wanted to ask your advice about something important."

"I'm better at lecturing than I am at giving advice, but I'll be glad to help if I can," Professor Shelby said and smiled.

Harley smiled back. She felt better already. Without fanfare, she said, "I'm thinking about traveling to India and I wanted to speak with you before I go."

Shelby's eyes grew wide and in a cheerful tone that sounded to Harley a bit contrived, he said, "I'm glad to learn someone in my class is influenced by the material I teach. And when exactly are you thinking of going?"

"Summer break," Harley replied. She felt that despite his tone, he was not happy with where the conversation seemed to be heading. Awkwardly, she looked around the room. On a chest of drawers by the window was a picture of Professor Shelby standing upright on a surfboard, his left hand raised triumphantly. He caught her staring at the picture and said, "Hawaii."

"I surf as well," Harley said proudly, glad they had a mutual interest to talk about.

"The best feeling in the world," he declared.

"As long as you look down the line," she said.

"I have yet to look at a wave without considering what it would be like to surf it and what my odds of doing so without crashing are."

She laughed out loud, relating to his words. Now that the tension was diffused, she felt it was the right moment to take a leap of faith.

"You and my mom attended the same college," she said.

Shelby nodded. "Yes, we went to school together, but we didn't keep in touch. I was happy to see her at the new students' orientation. She's a psychologist, right?"

Harley had no desire to discuss her mother's career; she was there to talk about Gangotri and determined to get back to the point of her visit.

"Yes," she replied to Professor Shelby's question, fixing her gaze directly at him. "But before she was a psychologist she traveled to India, and that's exactly what I intend to do."

Professor Shelby noted the confidence with which this young student carried herself. *A serious person*, he thought to himself. *A rare mix of bluntness and courage, qualities that reminded him of an old friend.*

"So where would you like to begin your trip to India? The Taj Mahal?"

"I was actually thinking I'd start at the Indian Himalayas, at one of the pilgrimage sites you mentioned in class." She hesitated for a moment, then added, "Maybe at a place like Gangotri."

Shelby's face turned a bit pale. Her answer took him off guard. Stiffly, he got up and stood by the window. Harley thought he suddenly looked older. Under his breath she could hear him mumble, "Gangotri, of all places . . ."

His voice grew quiet. It appeared his thoughts were somewhere else. He turned to Harley with a grave face. "Well, it's certainly an unconventional destination," he said. "Most travelers to India stick to the tourist sites, not venture to a place as remote and unruly as Gangotri." He gave her a stern look and added, "And it's dangerous to travel there alone. The Indian Himalayas are an unforgiving terrain."

Harley did not reply. This reaction certainly did not align with her perception of Professor Shelby as an adventurous explorer who encouraged his students to go out and see the world.

"Just out of curiosity," he asked, "why do you want to go there? Why don't you begin your travels in Delhi, Rajasthan, or Mumbai?"

"There's something mysterious about the whole story of the Ganges River and the journey to its source. I'm fascinated by it."

He nodded. "Yes, the Ganges is the world's holiest river. Indians believe it has flowed for eons." His tone shifted and Harley could tell he was putting on his lecturer persona, formal and distant. She pondered this sudden change. "For thousands of years, pilgrims bathed in its holy waters to purify themselves of wrong deeds or their poor fate . . ."

"So that's my point really. You've already traveled the world," she interrupted him. "Now it's my turn to . . ."

He didn't let her finish her sentence. "You have no idea what kind of trouble you could get yourself into. We are talking about a region with no medical facilities, where the conditions make an emergency evacuation by plane impossible, an area prone to avalanches, to dreadful blizzards."

"But you described the pilgrimage sites as the most exciting places in India!"

The professor turned toward a small cabinet, took out an expensive looking bottle of whiskey, poured some into a crystal glass and emptied it in one sip. Harley frowned, knowing that alcohol wasn't allowed in the university, but Shelby didn't seem to be bothered by this. He turned to her and spoke in a serious and tense voice.

"That was in class. I did not for a moment think someone would want to go there. Don't you realize I cannot allow myself to be responsible for such a trip?"

Harley did not respond. She nodded her head toward the professor and left his office without saying goodbye.

The next morning, while sitting in class, Harley's gaze landed on Divya, an Indian exchange student from New

Delhi, studying at Columbia for the semester. When she laughed, and she laughed often, the dimple on her left cheek made her look even more jovial. She was as energetic and exuberant as a child after devouring several chocolate bars. In an instant, a plan formed in Harley's mind. After class she approached Divya and asked if she would like to get coffee when they finished for the day. Divya happily agreed.

They sat at a small cafe. Harley ordered a double latte and Divya drank herbal tea. Cradling her warm mug in her hands, Harley listened to Divya tell her about a student she had met the previous week.

"Can you believe he has a motorcycle? Just like the last boyfriend I had in New Delhi. He even let me try to ride it," she said and laughed. "I began riding, and at first I was a bit wobbly. You should have seen his face when he thought I was going to knock over his precious bike!" she said and imitated an outraged expression.

Harley laughed. Divya's playfulness and ease were catching. Harley leaned forward and asked, "And what happened? Did you actually fall?"

"I learned how to ride in New Delhi. New York is a cakewalk for me," Divya said and winked.

Harley was growing fonder of her new friend by the minute. It appeared nothing in Divya's life was too complicated, and she wondered what her secret was. Divya felt the shift in Harley's mood. Her alert eyes looked at Harley inquisitively.

"Is everything alright?"

"Yes, I just don't know how to ask you something I've been thinking about for a while," Harley said.

"Is it about a guy you are seeing?" Divya's eyes brightened.

Harley noted that this was probably Divya's favorite topic of conversation.

"No, actually," Harley smiled. "It's about India."

"India?"

"I have always wanted to go there," Harley said with an inner passion that took even her by surprise, "but it is only now that I believe I can actually make it happen."

"Amazing!" Divya called out. A few heads in the small cafe turned toward them and the two girls laughed.

"Yes, but there is only one problem, and I am hoping you can help me with it," Harley told her friend.

Divya nodded attentively.

"My mom would never let me go on my own. I was thinking . . ."

"Come with me!" Divya completed Harley's thought. Her eyes shined. "We will have so much fun!"

"Wow," Harley said gratefully. The first phase of her plan was complete. "Maybe you can come over this weekend to meet my mom?"

"Sure, I'll be happy to," Divya said.

When Harley came home, her mother was reading a newspaper on the small sofa. At the sight of her daughter, she put the newspaper down. Harley approached and hugged her. She sat by her mother's side, breathing in the faint smell of perfume in her hair.

"I want your advice about something," she said to her mother. Her experience taught her this was the best approach. People liked to be consulted, to feel in control of the situation. Her mother smiled affectionately, waiting for her to speak.

"I don't know if you remember me telling you about Divya, the Indian exchange student that came to our university from New Delhi."

"Yes, vaguely," her mother replied.

"We've become really close friends. She is helping me understand Indian culture, their way of thinking, and I'm helping her get acclimated here in New York."

"Go on," said her mother.

"Anyway, Divya invited me to stay with her family in New Delhi for a few weeks during summer break, and I wanted to get your opinion."

Sarah's lips turned downward. She took a few deep breaths and looked out the window. Harley noted her hesitation.

"Mom, it will be a wonderful opportunity for me to see and experience things I've only read about so far. I'd be staying with Divya and her family and they would accompany me everywhere. I think it's a chance to have a totally safe adventure."

Her mother was only partially listening. Her heart was heavy with worry as she thought of her only child traveling all the way to India for the entire summer break. "Are you sure it's a good idea?" she asked, and immediately regretted a question that so clearly exposed her fears.

After a long, silent moment, Harley turned to her mother and said, "How do you feel about inviting Divya over on Sunday, so you could get to know her?"

After her husband had disappeared without a trace, Harley's mother vowed she would not overprotect her daughter. She knew she had to let Harley face the world on her own. Harley turned out to have a flair for adventure. Sarah had bitten her tongue when her daughter had begun to surf with a group of Long Island surfers, and later, when she decided to learn karate and competed in intense matches. Still, Sarah struggled to give this adventure her blessing. "I'm not sure," she finally replied to her daughter's question.

"I promise I'll look after myself," Harley said, looking directly into her mother's eyes. Her mother drank the rest of her coffee and stroked her daughter's hair.

That Sunday Divya came over. As soon as she entered the apartment it filled up with her youthful, jovial spirit and boundless energy. She hugged Harley's mother like an old friend, handed her a bouquet of flowers, and quickly walked up to the big picture window overlooking the Hudson River.

Harley's mother placed the flowers in a tall vase and filled it with water. She brought out tea and cookies and they all sat and discussed the differences between living in New York City and New Delhi.

"With an Indian restaurant around any block, I feel right at home," Divya said and smiled.

"I understand you are only here for a few months," said Harley's mother.

"Yes, I am going back in the summer and it would be great if Harley could come with me to New Delhi. I could show her all my favorite spots and she'd get to meet my family and friends. . ." Divya paused, sensing discomfort, then added, "You have nothing to worry about, Mrs. Green. I won't let Harley out of my sight for more than two minutes."

Harley laughed and her mother laughed with her. They continued talking about all the things the girls could do in India until the sun was in the middle of the sky. Divya peeked at her watch and said, "I have to meet some friends that are in town only for a short visit. I had a great time here."

Hugging Harley and her mother warmly, she said goodbye.

Harley stood by the windowsill. The sun colored her brown hair auburn and framed her face with light.

"What do you think about this trip to India now, Mom?" she asked.

Harley's mother looked at her and thought about how much she loved her, and about how much she looked like her father. She turned to her daughter, hugged her tightly, and said, "Why not? This is your time to explore the world and have exciting adventures."

Harley was elated with her mother's change of heart. Soon she would be hiking in the same mountains that her father had explored years ago. She knew it would be a long shot to find any clues about his dramatic disappearance, but her heart told her that this adventure had the potential to change her life.

CHAPTER 4

THE DAYS AND WEEKS SLOWLY passed. On the last day of class Harley looked around and noticed that the classroom was half empty. Most students seemed sleepy, and Professor Shelby also did not appear to be particularly focused. After summarizing the main lessons covered in his course, he went over a list of recommended summer readings and then took to his chair to survey his kingdom. He smiled to himself, stood up, and said, "I enjoyed my time with you, and I hope you also enjoyed your time with me. Have a fun summer break and try pondering the meaning of this sentence." Turning to the board, he wrote: 'Seek wonder in unexpected places.'

A few students dutifully copied the sentence into their notebooks. Harley looked at them in astonishment. Didn't they understand this was not something they were going to be tested on? Most students began to file out of the classroom. When Harley neared Professor Shelby's desk to say goodbye, he said, "I wanted to talk to you. Do you have time?"

"I don't want to argue about my trip to India. I appreciate your advice, but I've already made up my mind," Harley said.

"Got it," Professor Shelby said. "I won't mention India. But you did come to me for advice, and even though giving advice is not my specialty, I'd like to at least try."

"Advice about what?" Harley asked.

"Anything. Your future. I'm afraid I was no help at all the last time we spoke. Would you give me another opportunity?"

Harley silently followed him out of the classroom. Instead of heading to his office he suggested they take a walk through the park. "I've always maintained that fresh air sharpens the mind," he said and smiled.

Harley nodded in agreement. At the park, a few mothers were playing with their children. The trees were green and the breeze was pleasant. Two squirrels were chasing each other on a tall branch. They walked for a few minutes without speaking. Harley felt safe and calm with Professor Shelby despite their earlier disagreement about the possibility of her traveling to Gangotri. He treated her like an equal, unlike most other professors who spent their time trying to prove how smart they were, usually at the expense of the students who were paying to learn from them.

"You are now transitioning into a crucial stage in your life," Professor Shelby said.

"And I should focus on becoming a successful architect instead of wasting my time in the Himalayas?" Harley asked with a cynical smile.

"That's right" Shelby nodded his head. "I remember that in the first day of my class you mentioned that you were studying to become an architect but somehow found the time to enroll in a class about pilgrimage sites in India."

"There was something about the topic that drew me in," said Harley.

"Nothing wrong with that. Only you can decide what is the right path for you."

Harley's alert and intrigued look encouraged him to continue. "You are exactly at the stage where you have to learn to take big risks. Everything is possible. You have time to explore who you really are, plenty of time."

"I mean, everyone is exploring the world around them and trying to find what's right for them," Harley said.

"That's true," Shelby replied. "But the tragic mistake of most young people your age is that they don't search long and hard enough. What I'm talking about here is a search that could last a long time. Maybe even eighteen years," he said and smiled.

Harley furrowed her brow and said, "I don't know anyone my age who would be willing to spend so many years searching." She felt that there was some set doctrine behind Dr. Shelby's words. "Seems to me that you have a very different view of what I should do with my life than most adults I know."

"Well, it's not really a view of mine," he said. "It's a theory based on extensive research."

"What do you call this theory?"

"We called it the Principle of Eighteen, for we have found that if you take your entire lifetime and split it into five periods of eighteen years, each phase has a specific theme and focus to it. Leading a full life requires you to move from one phase to the next, always making changes at the eighteen-year marks."

"We?" asked Harley. "I thought it was your own theory?"

"No, there were three of us."

"And are you still working on this research today?"

He took a deep breath and said, "The group dismantled many years ago."

"And can't you get it back together?"

A shadow passed across Shelby's face and he decisively replied, "There is no possibility of that."

"So, what am I supposed to be doing at this stage of my life according to this principle?" Harley asked.

"Harley, do you know anything about the significance of the number eighteen?"

"Significance?" she repeated, not sure what he meant.

"The number eighteen is very special," Shelby said in a professorial voice. "In Judaism it represents the word *Hai*, which means "life." Jews believe eighteen represents the energy of our life. That's the origin of the custom of giving monetary gifts in multiples of eighteen: to confer a long life to the gift's recipient. In Japan it's linked to the essence of Buddhism since it is the product of six times three. The number six represents the six channels through which we experience the world: taste, smell, touch, sound, color, and justice." As he spoke, he counted with his fingers, then added three more. "And the number three represents the concepts of goodness, evil, and inner peace. And in China, the number eighteen is believed to bring special luck that can make you wealthy."

Harley wasn't sure she understood her professor's point. Her guard was up; she worried his miniature lecture would eventually lead to yet another reason she should avoid travelling to India.

They kept walking until they arrived at a large lake. Several white ducks sailed back and forth at the center of the lake and a warm wind whistled around them. Shelby pointed to a big wooden structure on the other side and Harley nodded in agreement. In silence, they circled half the lake until they made it to the wooden structure.

"Harley, so far you've dreamt about what you want to do and who you wish to be. Now it's time to follow those dreams, to search for the key to your happiness."

Harley tensed when she heard the word *key*; instinctively, her left hand reached for the pendant around her neck. She relaxed when her fingers met the small golden key.

"And what if I discover that what I dreamed is not what I want to do?"

"Excellent. It's best to find that out as soon as possible. Once you realize a certain dream is not right for you, or that you are not willing to sacrifice what it takes to make it come true, you have to start dreaming again about the type of person you could become in the future."

"That can take . . ." she paused as she considered the path of the dreamer, then completed the sentence, "an awfully long time,"

"As I mentioned, yes, a long time," he said and nodded. "Most of us don't dedicate the proper time for it. We pay the price for that later."

Harley said nothing and Shelby repeated his words. "I believe you should dedicate yourself to the search, no matter how long it takes."

"Even if it takes several years?"

"Yes," he answered definitively. "What really stops us from discovering our destiny in life is that we are afraid to be different from everyone else. We believe we should just toe the line and follow the paved road laid out in front of us. During your search you begin to understand yourself in a deeper way. You start making decisions that are right for you, even if they go against the expectations of those who love you."

Shelby's words struck a powerful chord in Harley's soul. There was something subversive in what he was saying, not rebellion for rebellion's sake, but a genuine desire to make young people such as herself see their true nature.

She turned to Shelby and said, "I think most people don't ask themselves what they can amount to and just get carried away with the flow of life."

"That's accurate," Shelby agreed. "Instead of going after their dreams they fulfill other people's desires and ambitions without even being aware of it. The problem starts when they suddenly wake up in the middle of their lives and realize how much time they've wasted on insignificant things."

"Is it too late for them?" Harley wondered.

"It's never too late," Shelby replied. "It's just harder. Realizing that for most of your life you've been guided by other people is hard to process. If you don't know how to move past that realization, feelings of regret could easily turn you into a bitter person."

Harley nodded and swore to herself she would never get to that point.

"And what happens after I've explored my dreams? What do I have to do then?"

They turned onto a shaded path that was empty of people. The sound of children at play was now distant and dim. After a few minutes Shelby said, "You have to make a plan for the next stage and act on it. But that will come later. Right now, you need to believe in yourself, in your ability to get up every time and face what life has in store for you."

Harley looked at him and thought that he had given up on himself and was now trying to save her. She was touched by this. Smiling at him, she said, "I promise you I don't intend on giving up any time soon. I don't know exactly what I'm searching for, but I know it must be something bigger than chasing money and prestige. I just know there is something beyond that, something wonderful that can fill one's life with beauty and warmth."

Professor Shelby smiled at the girl's hopefulness. "Like you, I wanted to understand what the best way to live my life was . . ." His voice faded as he continued thinking of his youth, the innocence and enthusiasm he had lost over the years. "It's been so long since then . . . now, when I'm in my mid-fifties, you could say I've forgotten what I'm really looking for."

"I won't let that happen to me," Harley said confidently. "You don't have to worry."

"I wish that for you with all my heart," Shelby said. "You never know in life. Some people get up and move forward after each blow, but most of us . . ."

"Get tired and give up," Harley completed his sentence.

They passed under a gigantic oak tree and sat on a bench beneath it. The sun was mid-sky and Harley enjoyed its pleasant warmth all over her body. She felt a type of pleasant weariness and considered how nice it would be to fall into a light slumber, just like that, in the middle of the day, on a park bench. She heard birds chirping, peered into the tree above, and saw a yellow- breasted bird on a faraway branch, staring into the distance. After a minute or two it flew on her way without a sound. She glanced at Professor Shelby and saw that his gaze was also focused somewhere on the horizon. He noticed her glance, cleared his throat, and said, "It's easier than you think to lose sight of your dreams when you are faced with crises."

He fell silent and she did not interrupt his thoughts. It seemed he was at a loss for words, but after a few moments he continued talking.

Sitting up straight, he said, "What's interesting to see is that the heart never forgets our dreams. We can build high walls, surround these walls with armed watchmen, but messages from the heart still find a way in."

"And how do we communicate with these messengers?"

"Usually, they appear in our dreams while the guards' control loosens a bit."

Harley immediately recalled her dream about her father in the ice cave. She cleared her throat and said, "Recently I had a strange dream. I feel that there is a hidden, powerful message within this dream, but I can't seem to grasp it."

He chuckled and said, "Trying to interpret dreams is a complicated business. People greater than myself have written hefty books on the subject, but I am not sure those can help you much."

"Are you suggesting I ignore these dreams?"

"Not at all. What matters is how they make you feel."

"I feel that I'm fighting for my life, like someone running down a narrow and dark alley, trying to outrun something frighteningly evil. The alley might lead to a dead end, but there is also a sliver of hope that it could lead me to a sunny seaport, where I have a boat waiting to whisk me away to a wonderful place."

Shelby smiled and said, "That's nice imagery. Rilke, the German poet, said that 'our deepest fears are like . . .'"

". . . dragons guarding our deepest treasure,'" Harley said, completing his sentence.

They both laughed at this shared knowledge. Harley loved this image. In her mind she saw two mighty purple-and-crimson dragons guarding a cave at the top of a towering cliff, shrouded by thick fog. Shelby said something, but she listened with only one ear, focusing instead on the image of the dragons. Two grown men in sweats slowly ran past them. Harley noticed one of the runners was dragging his left foot a little, but that this did not stop him from keeping the same pace as his friend.

She and Professor Shelby arose and continued walking until they had reached a short path leading up to Fifth Avenue. Shelby stopped and turned to Harley,

"About Gangotri . . ." Shelby began to say.

She gave him a harsh stare.

Professor Shelby shook his head. "Let me try again. What I mean to say is, like everyone, I too went through something that affected me deeply."

Harley was surprised he was opening to her. Her face took on a serious expression as she listened.

"It was many years ago, and it still dominates my thoughts. Not a day goes by when I don't think about it." He lowered his head.

Harley felt an urge to ask him what the "it" was but held herself back. Shelby seemed to be revealing to her a fragment of his soul, and she needed to proceed carefully.

"Why are you telling me this?" Harley asked tenderly.

"One thing that I have learnt from my experience is that you shouldn't let anything, or anyone, make you lose sight of what your heart tells you to do."

Harley gave Professor Shelby a quick piercing glance and nodded. She sensed that he seemed somewhat surprised by his own advice. They walked silently until they arrived at the Fifth Avenue exit, where they said goodbye.

CHAPTER 5

A WEEK LATER HARLEY DECIDED to visit Uncle Charlie, her brother's father, who lived in an enormous mansion in Westchester, about an hour from New York City. Charlie was her father's younger and only brother, but her mother had not kept in touch with him. Harley knew that Charlie's name was tied to a few corruption scandals. News of this had appeared in the papers some years back, but that didn't stop her from reaching out. She knew he had organized a search party after her father's disappearance and was eager to find out if he would share any information he might previously have kept to himself. She dialed his number and spoke to Mary, the housekeeper, who told her Charlie would be delighted to see her.

Late on a rainy and foggy afternoon, Harley boarded a train from Grand Central Station. Strong winds were blowing outside, and she bundled herself up in her warm coat as she thought about the upcoming encounter. From the Westchester station, she took a taxi, which dropped her off at the opening of a dense forest. Harley paid and thanked the driver, then began walking toward the mansion. Wet leaves stuck to her shoes and the air smelled refreshingly of rain. She walked along a winding rocky path until she saw the mansion, a gigantic structure designed to look like a medieval fort. A long water canal surrounded it and three tall spires towered above it in chilling silence. The sun pierced through the clouds, casting the mansion in a golden light. Stepping across a wooden bridge over the canal, Harley saw fat goldfish swimming back and forth in the clear water. Beautiful lilies rose from the water and leaves from the last storm gracefully littered its surface.

At the entrance, a stocky security guard with a rough pockmarked face appeared out of nowhere. He inquired who she was and relayed her response through a two-way radio. After receiving a reply, he gestured toward a vast staircase leading to a wide heavy door. Harley climbed the stairs and rang the doorbell. Mary the housekeeper, a portly, amiable woman, opened the door. At seeing Harley, she gave her a warm hug.

"You've gotten so big; I just can't believe it!" Mary exclaimed. "Look at you, who would have imagined you'd turn into such a beautiful girl?"

Harley smiled, embarrassed.

"Charlie is waiting for you in the study."

They mounted a great stairwell made of burnished mahogany. A round chandelier hung above them, emanating a pleasant yellow light. After they crossed a long high-ceilinged hallway, they ascended a curved flight of stairs to arrive at a thick oak door. Mary grasped the round iron knocker at the center of the door and knocked.

"Come in," a voice said from inside.

The door opened into a massive round room with an even taller ceiling. Sunshine entered through skylights and circles of light flickered onto tall golden-brown shelves, which contained hundreds of art books. Charlie sat in his favorite brown leather armchair—a fancy piece of furniture that must have weighed a ton. When he saw Harley, he rose from his seat with some effort and a smile. Harley noticed grey peppering his red beard and mustache, and a small potbelly that had sprouted since she'd seen him last. He opened his arms and they embraced.

"I'll get you something to drink," Mary said.

"You look great," he said.

"And I see you've put on some weight," she said and smiled.

"Mary's cooking," he laughed, and then asked Harley, "By the way, how's your mother these days?"

"Fine, as usual," she said. "You two don't really keep in touch, huh?" she added.

"Your mother believes everything she reads in the papers," said Charlie. "I had nothing to do with the scandal involving the congressman and the real estate deal."

Harley glanced around the palatial room and said nothing. She took a deep breath and said, "Charlie, I want to know what exactly happened to my Dad in India."

Charlie turned his gaze to the wood burning in the large fireplace. He stuffed his pipe and exhaled some puffs of smoke. Red-and-orange flames flickered against the walls of the fireplace and the wood softly crackled. He said in a quiet voice, "When the accident happened, I felt I should have looked after him better, even though he was a grown man responsible for his own actions. Still . . ." He let out another puff of sweet smoke into the large space.

"I arranged a professional rescue team as soon as your mother told me he was missing. His last known location was a place called Gangotri, somewhere deep in the Indian Himalayas. From what I could gather, he was trying to get to a remote ice cave that is the source of the Ganges River."

Harley hid her excitement and nodded. "Mom told me you made a huge effort to find him, to no avail."

"They found nothing. Your father simply disappeared off the face of the earth."

"There were no clues? No leads?"

Charlie got up from his seat and walked toward a writing desk made from a tree trunk whose surface was concentric circles. He opened one of the drawers and pulled out a yellowing piece of paper in a clear plastic binder.

"That's the official report I got from the head of the rescue team." He took out the report and start reading out loud.

"After an extensive search, we have found no conclusive evidence that will shed light on what happened to Jack

Green. Aside from a record of a night stay at Gangotri, we were not able to find any guide that accompanied Mr. Green to the glacier. At the time of his disappearance, there were deep fissures within the glacier, some up to fifty feet in depth, and many of these fissures were covered in bottomless snow. Our assumption is that Jack Green fell into one of the crevices in the glacier."

Charlie handed Harley the report. A handwritten comment at the edge of the note drew her attention. "One of the pilgrims said a man matching Jack's description was seen on his way to the glacier with another person. We were unable to corroborate that testimony." Another comment in red below this line read: "Probably a case of mistaken identity."

"You think there was someone else with him?" Harley asked in an excited tone.

"I have tried for years to look for a lead that would solve this mystery. I even offered a substantial reward to anyone who could provide any reliable information about Jack," said Charlie.

"And what happened?" Harley asked.

"What happened? There was a traveling parade of treasure seekers, gold diggers, and scam artists. The reward is still on the table, but no one has been able to shed light on what really happened to your father."

Harley nodded her head. Soon Mary entered, holding a bamboo tray with two mugs, a pitcher of tea, and fresh butter cookies. She placed the tray on a round table near them and exited without a word.

"I am going to India for a few weeks," Harley said, taking a sip of the tea and trying to sound casual. "I'll be staying with a classmate's family."

At this news, Charlie raised his eyebrows. "And what does your mother have to say about this adventurous trip?" he asked.

Harley cleared her throat. "She's not wild about the idea, but I got her blessing."

Charlie rose from his seat with a slight sigh, approached the writing desk again, opened the top drawer, and pulled out an elegant black leather wallet. He held the wallet in his left hand as if weighing it, then turned it over and with his right hand removed a faded photograph with yellow margins. As he looked at the photograph, his hand quivered. Harley approached and was surprised to see the same photograph she had hanging above her bed, the one showing her smiling father with a Sherpa against the backdrop of the Himalayan Mountains.

Harley put her hand on Uncle Charlie's shoulder and said, "You once told me you two had a unique bond."

"You remind me so much of him," he replied, tears filling his eyes. "When you are here, it's as if he is in the room with us . . ."

Charlie returned to the writing desk. He rummaged for a moment in one of the drawers, then pulled out a thick envelope. After sizing up its weight, he handed it to Harley.

"A little something from me to help you in the near future."

Harley opened the envelope. It was full of cash. She quickly handed it back. "I can't take this," she said.

Charlie chuckled. "Just like your mother," he said. "You do know, don't you, that I offered to pay for your college and your mother adamantly refused?"

Harley said nothing. She remembered the firm objection of her mother, who preferred to take out long-term loans to fund her daughter's education. Harley studied the flames that were making intricate shapes on the fireplace walls for a few minutes until realizing that she doesn't want to act like her mother. She accepted the envelope and with a steady voice said, "Thanks, Charlie. I really appreciate your help."

Together they walked through the mansion to its front door. At the entrance, Charlie clasped her niece's shoulders. "Promise your old uncle one thing."

"I'm listening," Harley said.

"Don't put yourself in danger. If achieving the goal you set for yourself involves risking your life, give up and just head back."

Harley wondered if her uncle had guessed what she was planning to do, but his expression was sealed. Hugging him tightly, she said, "I promise."

Once outside again, she began walking along the winding rocky path. When she rounded the bend in the road that obscured the mansion, she turned back and saw Uncle Charlie following her with his eyes, pipe in hand. The fading sun created a long shadow next to him, and for a minute Harley could see the tall figure of her father, hugging his little brother and waving her goodbye.

CHAPTER 6

HARLEY COULD NOT FALL ASLEEP the night before her flight to India. She turned on the night lamp by her bed and read again the travel guide she had bought. With a sharp pencil, she marked the path she would take from New Delhi to Rishikesh at the foot of the Himalayas. She circled the tiny dot of Gangotri, where roads ended, and towering mountains harbored her father's secret. Eventually she managed to fall asleep.

When she woke up, she smelled an appetizing, familiar smell. She opened her door and saw that her mother had made a fresh pot of coffee and her favorite pancakes. She felt her eyes beginning to water. She gently closed her door, walked to the bathroom, and splashed her face with cold water. Afterward, she joined her mother for breakfast.

When they had finished eating, her mother reached down and pulled a thin pouch tied with long lace from her purse. Harley examined the pouch. It had a single, nylon-padded compartment that closed when its two sides were pinned together.

"I bought this for you, for the trip. I want you to keep your money in this pouch, along with your passport and plane tickets. It's waterproof, too."

Harley pouted her lips and raised a skeptical eyebrow.

But her mother insisted. "I once made a journey like this myself. That was many years ago, but I don't believe things have changed all that much."

"I know how to look out for myself," Harley said, and raised her head defiantly.

"Yes, here in New York. But you are traveling to a different world now." She placed the pouch around her daughter's neck and said, "Don't ever part with this pouch, not even when you go to sleep."

Harley thought her mom was overdoing it, but she remained silent. It was time to say goodbye. Her mother looked at her and hugged her tightly. "Keep your cool and you'll see that everything will be alright."

Harley smiled; only her mother could say goodbye to her in this way. Everyone who knew Sarah knew that she never wallowed in self-pity or lamented her sad fate. She had raised Harley on her own, worked a full-time job, and kept her moments of struggle to herself. Harley admired her, but often had a hard time talking to her for it sometimes seemed she was made of steel.

A few minutes and one last hug later Harley headed to the airport. At the departures hall she met Divya, and the girls embraced warmly, happy to see each other. Once they boarded the plane, Harley felt a quiver of excitement rush through her body. She closed her eyes for a moment and thought—*Here I go*. Sensing her friend's jitteriness, Divya gently touched the palm of her hand. Harley opened her eyes.

"Is everything alright?" Divya asked.

Harley nodded.

"You're with me and I promise you everything is going to be fine," Divya assured her.

Something about her openness moved Harley. Without giving it a second thought, she said, "You know, there's something I haven't yet told you."

Divya looked at her with curious black eyes. She pushed her long straight hair to the side and said eagerly, "Does it have to do with one of the boys in class?"

"Not at all," Harley laughed heartily. Then she grew serious and said, "The real reason for this trip has to do with my past, my childhood." She coughed twice, swallowed hard and said, "Remember you asked me about my father, and I told you he doesn't live with us?"

Divya nodded.

"I lied to you. I didn't have the guts to tell you the truth. Eight years ago, my dad went on a trek in the Himalayas, to a place called Gangotri, on the way to the source of the Ganges River."

"I remember that place from Dr. Shelby's lecture," Divya said, leaning forward with interest.

Harley exhaled and said, "He never made it back from there. He disappeared eight years ago and my mother's life and mine have been upside down ever since."

Divya stared at Harley for a long moment and eventually said, in a tone of admiration and puzzlement, "You're planning to look for him . . ."

Harley nodded. "My uncle organized a search team, but they came back empty-handed. He simply disappeared off the face of the earth . . ."

Divya shook her head and said softly, "Thanks for sharing that with me. I promise you no one will ever know about it."

Harley gave her a grateful look. They were both silent for a while. Divya was the first to speak. "You know, I just want to make sure you're prepared for disappointment," she gently said. "You must have thought about it—more than eight years have passed, and going on such a journey without any preparation, in the hope of finding something. . ."

Harley's heart sank when she heard what she was afraid to say herself. She thought of all the ways she was putting herself at risk and of the incredibly slim odds of discovering anything of value. Divya realized Harley was not about to break her deep silence.

"I don't want to be the one pouring cold water, but it is best to hear this now and think about it before you are in the middle of the trek and can't go back. If you decide to do this, I'll help you, but don't forget I promised your mother I was going to look out for you."

Harley found Divya's sudden seriousness moving. "Don't worry," Harley assured her, "I intend to look out for myself and not do anything stupid."

"I'd come with you," Divya said, "but I don't have your sense of adventure. We all have to know our limitations." She sat up straight in her seat and repeated her promise, "But I'll help you any way I can. My father has excellent connections at an ashram in Haridwar, he can point you in the right direction," she smiled broadly and said, "I think it's simply amazing that you're doing this, no matter what you discover!"

The flight went by quickly and in the late afternoon they landed in New Delhi. The airport was crowded and bustling. At the bank, Harley exchanged her dollars for rupees. She tried putting all her money inside the pouch around her neck, but the bills made it heavy and cumbersome. She took some of the money from the pouch and stashed it in her backpack. Hand in hand, she and Divya exited the airport. It was early evening, and a big red sun could be seen from afar. The air was heavy with smog, and Harley coughed, trying to get used to the suffocating pollution.

People were swarming everywhere; a warm wind blew, and the sky was grey and metallic. Rain began to pour. Harley tried to seek shelter but Divya grabbed her arm and walked with her toward an older man in a suit standing by a shiny black car. The driver took their luggage and opened the car door. They sat in the back, relieved to finally be at their destination after their long flight.

It was hot and humid, and the driver turned on the air conditioning. Through the car's tinted windows, Harley could not see much. She felt she was inside a bubble protecting her from the outside world. Occasionally when the car stopped, she could make out the fuzzy faces of children carrying things and knocking on the car doors. The traffic was slow, the rundown roads full of bumps and potholes. Motorcycles, rickshaws, trucks, and pedestrians surrounded them everywhere. After what felt like forever, they arrived in a neighborhood of beautiful well-kept houses. The driver entered the garage of one of these houses, turned off the engine, and opened the car door for them.

The family was waiting for them outside: Divya's mother, a cheerful woman in an orange-green sari; her father, a distinguished looking man with a long narrow face and thin glasses; and her two little brothers who seemed to be about seven years old, dressed in sportswear. After they had exchanged warm hugs with Divya, her mother opened her arms to Harley.

"Welcome to our home," the mother said in melodic English and with a radiant smile. "Divya has told us so many things about you."

Harley blushed and smiled in embarrassment. The father turned to the girls. "You must be tired from your long trip. Let's have a drink in the guest room."

The house was large and well lit. Art graced the walls in the form of spectacular paintings of gods, elephants, and tigers. Harley felt as if she were in a museum. They sat in the guest room and an elderly maid served them a cold and delicious yogurt drink. Divya and her two little brothers played on a big green carpet, wrestling and laughing. Harley watched them and thought about how different her life could have been if she were not an only child. Opening her backpack, she pulled out two blue toy cars she had brought. The twin boys shyly approached her and waited for their mother's approval before accepting the presents. After the mother nodded, they reached out with their little brown arms toward Harley, who gave them the presents with a smile. Their black eyes brightened as they said thank you in perfect English.

"Thank you for Gauri and Samir's presents," the mother said with a smile.

"It's the least I could do," Harley replied, smiling back. She felt right at home with this Indian family. They let her feel that she could act naturally without being judged. Meanwhile, Divya started to unpack one of her suitcases, handing her own gifts to her family. The father turned to his daughter and said with a smile in his eyes, "Is there anything left in New York you didn't manage to buy?"

Divya began to tell them about all her experiences abroad, and the adoring parents hung on her every word. Harley felt sleep overtaking her. A fight between the twins upstairs and her friend's melodic voice filtered through to her as if through a pleasant dream. The armchair she sat on was so comfortable. *I must find a way to get to Gangotri*, she thought to herself; but thinking about everything she had to do to arrive at her destination made her even more tired. Divya's mother noticed Harley nodding off. Interrupting her daughter's stream of words, she said, "Divya, Harley looks exhausted. Why don't you take her upstairs to her room and we'll continue talking later?"

Harley said good night to the parents and went up to the second floor. Her room was large, with a vast window overlooking the lush garden and a shiny mahogany desk. In the middle of the room was a wide bed and above it a photograph of a herd of elephants heading toward a brook in the early morning.

"I am sure you'll sleep well tonight. If you need me, I'll be in the next room," Divya said and hugged her good night. Harley thanked her and then closed the door. Too tired to shower, Harley settled on washing her face and changing into her pajamas. Snuggling in the soft blanket, she thought how exciting life can be. She felt lucky to be there, in this strange place, so far from her home and her normal life. "Everything is going to be alright," she said to herself over and over, before falling into a deep, dreamless sleep.

Soft sunlight entered the open blinds and gently woke Harley. Birds were chirping outside. She thought she saw a monkey through the window and told herself she must still be dreaming. Getting out of bed, she walked to the window and saw that a monkey was, in fact, sitting on a branch outside her room. Harley opened the window wide but the monkey, casting her an almost human look, did not move from its place. She heard a knock on the door. When she opened it, a short maid was smiling at her with a breakfast tray that included a cold yogurt drink, freshly baked almond cookies, and peeled apples. Harley ate with relish, knowing that these kinds of treats would be rare during her adventure.

After she dressed, her eyes landed on the pouch hanging from the windowsill. Her mother's cautioning voice echoed in her ears even though Harley wished she could ignore it. Hastily, she hid the pouch under the mattress and then went downstairs. Divya and her family smiled affectionately at her. They were again sitting in the guest room. Through the large windows the garden surrounding the house was in clear view. Harley saw swaying palm trees, tall green bushes, and colorful flowers decorating the edges of the garden. Several monkeys hung on the branches and invisible birds chirped their songs.

"You seem to have recovered after a good night's sleep," Divya's father said with a smile.

"I feel like a totally different person," Harley replied.

One of the twins shyly approached her with the red toy car.

"I think Gauri wishes to play with you," Divya laughed.

Harley followed Gauri to a long sunlit balcony. The little boy sat on the floor and when Harley sat next to him, he motioned her to sit farther away. From the other end of the balcony, she grabbed the blue car, spun it, and sent it speeding back. A light breeze blew between the treetops. She played with Gauri until Divya came and called her back to the guest room. When Harley got up to leave, Gauri smiled at her affectionately, like someone who had just found a new friend. She stroked his head.

The father turned to Harley. "Do you know what you wish to do in New Delhi or are you going to let Divya take you to her usual hangouts?"

"I think I'll just trust Divya," Harley said and smiled. She wanted to start planning her real adventure but knew she first had to go into the city. She went up to her room to get ready.

When she opened the door, her face dropped. The window was wide open and leftovers from breakfast were scattered everywhere. Her backpack had been thrown aside to one corner of the room, and everything she had brought with her to India was tossed about. The room appeared as if a gang of thieves had meticulously ransacked it.

She looked for her toiletry bag and couldn't find it. *Who would want to steal such a thing?* she wondered. Suddenly she remembered the money pouch under the mattress. Her heart was pounding as she moved the pile of things on the bed and lifted the mattress. The pouch was there. She let out a sigh of relief, put the pouch around her neck, and promised herself that from now on and until the end of her journey she would always wear it.

She ran downstairs and told the family what had happened. Divya asked her if she had left the window open and when Harley replied that she had, she looked at her with a sympathetic smile and told her the monkeys wait for exactly this kind of opportunity.

"They usually search for food, but they can also steal the very thing you care about the most."

Harley told her she had seen a monkey in the morning and Divya nodded. "He was simply scouting the area. He saw you had just arrived and took advantage of the situation." They went up to the bedroom and Divya clicked her tongue at the sight of the damage. She called the maid in, but Harley insisted on cleaning everything up herself.

Over the following days, Divya and Harley toured New Delhi's main sites. They hung out with Divya's friends at the Red Fort, had a picnic dinner near the India Gate, and spent time at Connaught Place—New Delhi's leisure district.

Throngs of people, ancient structures, monkeys, and cows were everywhere, and the noise and commotion that were an inseparable part of New Delhi charmed and tired Harley in equal measure. Harley felt she could spend the entire trip in this captivating city but knew she had to begin her journey to Gangotri. Divya had told her that her father had excellent connections at an ashram in Haridwar, a small town near Rishikesh. Harley thought she could use those connections to make up a story the father would believe about why she wished to travel near the mountains.

During the family dinner Harley asked Divya's father if he knew any ashrams in Rishikesh. His eyes lit up. He told her Rishikesh was known as the world's yoga capital and that pilgrims came to it every year to bathe in the holy Ganges River. "In fact, the Ganges River is considered the holiest in three places—Rishikesh, Haridwar, and Gangotri. People arrive from across India to those places to bathe in the river and take holy water with them back home," he said.

Harley's heart skipped a beat when he mentioned the name Gangotri.

"Why are you interested in an ashram?" he gently asked.

"I would like to experience real meditation," Harley replied, attempting to sound sincere. "Not something you do for a few hours, but a weeklong program, or even longer."

Divya added, "Harley wants to be introduced to everything we have to offer, not just the shopping centers and other distractions of New Delhi." She winked at Harley and her parents smiled and nodded.

Admiringly, the father said, "Good, very good. But Rishikesh is too crowded. You must go to a quieter place at the foot of the Himalayas, a small town named Haridwar. Haridwar is considered a gate to the gods, especially to the God Vishnu. It's the last place at the foot of the Himalayas before the Ganges River begins curving downward. We believe Vishnu scattered drops of a potion there that guarantees eternal youth, and that bathing in Haridwar helps wash away your sins before your next incarnation."

Harley remembered from the maps she had learned by heart that Haridwar was an excellent point of departure for the Himalayan Mountains. She felt her heart beating faster.

The father added, "I took such a course a few years ago at Babaji's ashram in Haridwar. I'll give you a letter for Babaji and our driver can take you to the bus station as soon as you are ready. The bus will take you to Rishikesh and from there any rickshaw driver can take you to the bridge leading to Haridwar."

Without delay the father wrote a brief letter and gave it to Harley. She nearly jumped for joy but knew it would be rude to leave right away, as much as she wanted to. She thanked him profusely. Divya smiled affectionately at her and Harley thought how great it was to be sharing her secret with such a loyal and discreet ally. After thanking everyone, she went up to her room. In an external pocket of her backpack, she placed the letter she just received from Divya's father along with her father's last letter to her from Gangotri. She then called her mother and told her that everything was fine. Harley detected both relief and stress in her mother's voice. She told her mother she was about to take a weeklong meditation course in which she was expected to observe a vow of silence. Harley felt a bit guilty for continuing to lie to her mother, but she also noticed she was beginning to get used to these lies; they were becoming a part of her.

She spent the following day preparing for her bus ride to Rishikesh. Divya told her she would have to take the night bus from New Delhi's central train station and that she would arrive at the Ganges River at dawn. In the evening, to the chirping of birds outside, she said goodbye to the family. The father shook her hand, Divya and her mother gave her a warm hug. Little Gauri, holding the blue car, looked at her with concern, as if wondering if she would make it back safely. She thanked everyone and began to tear up as she entered the big black car. Outside, it started to drizzle.

The family's quiet driver brought her to the bus station. Harley thanked him and boarded an old bus. The night ride would take her to the town of Rishikesh at the foot of the Himalayas—her first stop on her way to Gangotri.

CHAPTER 7

THERE WERE NO OTHER TOURISTS on the bus, and it seemed that all the passengers were on their way to the holy Ganges. Her seat had seen better days. Metal springs stuck out from one of its sides and the grey fabric was full of patches and holes. She tried reclining a little but gave up after a few attempts. Outside the bus window, New Delhi was asleep, the incessant commotion of the daytime hours replaced with the slow rhythm of the night. Harley saw entire families camped out on the side of the road, their faces partially lit by dim streetlamps; packs of dogs running after the bus; and rickshaw drivers standing at street corners, leaning on their vehicles as they smoked.

After about an hour the bus exited New Delhi. It was pitch-black outside, but for occasional twinkles of light emanating from makeshift dwellings on the side of the road. Lost in thought, Harley absentmindedly played with the small golden key around her neck. Suddenly she felt another passenger's eyes on her and turned to see an older man with a potbelly and piercing eyes, staring. He was unshaven and his T-shirt, printed with a picture of an eagle soaring above a green valley, was oil stained.

Meeting her eyes, while pointing at his neck right at the spot where her key was dangling, the man whispered in English, "Do you want to know what's the key to happiness?"

Harley looked at the blackness outside the window. The man whispered something else in the dark space of the bus. Certain he was one of those countless beggars she saw on the streets, she ignored him. Moving to the seat next to hers, he gave her that same serious stare. She felt his breath on her neck and flinched.

"Would you like to know or not?"

This time his question was asked with a sense of urgency. Harley realized he was not going to give up.

"Sure," she shrugged, while fingering the small golden key around her neck.

The man pointed to the key. "That's a nice trinket you have there, but not the kind of key you need."

Gathering up the courage, Harley turned and said, "What makes you think I need anything?"

"You're on a bus of pilgrims heading to Rishikesh, aren't you?"

Harley considered the question. "Let's say I am looking for something. Why do you think you can help me?"

The man raised his hands and said, "It is my duty to share this knowledge with other path seekers. I didn't make up the rules, they were made a long time ago by people whose wisdom we can't even comprehend. Once you know where to find the key you must share that knowledge with as many people as possible." He lowered his voice while nodding his head from side to side. "But most people are not interested in searching for the thing that can set them free." He placed his hands over his wide chest. "Deep inside a person knows that if they stop and ask themselves the truly important questions, like what are we doing here, and why do we work so hard when every day is like the next, then they'd be forced to change their current lives."

Harley was suddenly all ears. "But what exactly are they missing out on in life?" she asked.

The man smiled. "The real key opens a door to incredible treasures, to truths that can make every person filled with joy for the rest of their life."

Harley thought for a moment, then said, "If you know where one can find such a key, why are you not surrounded by people asking how to find it?"

Shaking his head, the man said, "I already told you—no one believes it exists. And even if they did, they wouldn't want to commit."

"Commit to what?"

"To the universe. There are cosmic rules you must live by." With his finger, the man drew a circle in the air. "They are around you all the time, but if you don't learn how to recognize them, they will pass you by."

Harley followed the man's circular motions hypnotically but felt that the conversation itself was going in circles. Cosmic rules? She didn't have a clue what that meant.

Sensing her frustration, the man clarified. "The golden key is accessible to everyone. It's made from pure gold so that you can quickly identify it. From the moment you use it, you'll be on the path to happiness."

Harley was still skeptical. "And where exactly can you find this key?" she asked.

"At the bottom of a windswept lake, high in the mountains."

Harley imagined Gangotri's glacier, and her heart pounded.

The man cautioned, "The winds there are very strong, and prevent you from seeing what's in the lake."

Harley imagined diving into a freezing, murky lake that was at the mercy of icy winds. They were both quiet for a while. Eventually she asked the man where this lake was located. Passing over a rickety bridge, the bus swayed from side to side. The man got on his feet, gripped the back of the seat for support and said, "First you have to stop those winds from blowing."

Someone at the back of the bus was passing around a bag of chapatis. Harley's conversational partner was now devoted to the location of the thin Indian bread, rather than to the lake, and it seemed he had forgotten the question she had asked him. He went back to his original seat just in time to snag the last chapati and began eating it without giving Harley a second glance.

The beat-up bus continued its night journey, creaking loudly whenever it hit a pothole along the rundown road. Suddenly Harley heard a dull thud. The bus squealed and stopped. Passengers were tossed around everywhere. Harley was thrown forward and her head hit the back of the seat in front of her. Touching her forehead, she felt a painful bruise. She looked back and saw her former conversational partner moaning and holding his wrist. Murmurs passed through the bus like a wave. The driver got off the bus, accompanied by a few passengers.

Harley saw them arguing loudly. A crowd of people appeared out of nowhere. Gesticulating wildly, the driver tried to explain what had happened. He kept pointing to the bus, as if accusing it of the accident. Some of the passengers defended the driver, forming a human shield around him. Harley saw a few people lift an old woman into their arms and place her at the side of the road.

"The bus hit and killed her," her former conversational partner said. He was now back in the seat next to hers. "She simply crossed the road at the wrong place and the wrong time. It was her destiny."

"But she's dead," Harley replied, distraught.

"I hope her next incarnation will be a good one," he said while examining his wrist, turning it from side to side.

"Is it broken?" Harley asked with concern.

"It might be, but it's only the body," said the man. "There are two states in life. You're either alive or dead. If you're dead, nothing can be done. But if you're alive, you're lucky, and you must learn to never pity yourself. Self-pity will kill you faster than any injury."

The driver returned to the bus and continued his way as if nothing had happened. Harley didn't know what to make of this strange new world, where death and injury were both greeted with resignation.

But now all of that was behind her. She looked at the bridge and the sickening feeling from losing her backpack hit her again. *How could I be so stupid?* Harley wondered, recalling the chain of events that had started with the rickshaw driver who had picked her up after she plunged her head into the Ganges River. Following that, she had gotten out of the rickshaw to observe the magnificent bridge, momentarily forgetting about her backpack. The sad story ended with the rickshaw driver taking off with all her belongings. *There were so many opportunities for me along the way to avoid this situation*, she thought.

She stood up, touched the pouch around her neck and her small golden key, and recalled her mother's warning. *At least I have not lost everything*, she thought. This thought cheered her up and she began walking toward the bridge.

The bridge turned out to be a favorite hangout for the people of Haridwar. Every corner was densely occupied. Monkeys ran around it, climbing the long metal cables and jumping from side to side; cows stood idly in the middle; and gangs of children ran back and forth. It was also full of beggars and vendors hawking sugared candy and colorful powders in flat containers. Harley began to make her way across the bridge. While trying to avoid a cow standing in the middle of her path, she bumped into a yellow wooden crate and lost her balance. Mid-fall, someone grabbed her and steadied her into a sitting pose.

Lifting her eyes, she saw a wrinkled woman, her clothes dirtied by dust and mud. Several cards with strange images were scattered around her. Harley recognized Ganesh, the elephant god, on one of the cards, sitting cross-legged on a pedestal, his long trunk adorned with flowers. Before she could thank her, the woman grabbed Harley's hand and examined her palm, mumbling incomprehensible words to herself.

After a few moments she looked up and uttered a few sentences in quick Hindi. Harley raised her palms and shook her head. A few small children had gathered around them. One of them, scrawny with fiery eyes, translated the fortune-teller's words into English.

"You no die now . . . only old woman . . ." he said. "Big house . . . green country . . . good money." The other children clapped upon hearing the good news. Harley smiled politely. "Three children: two girls, one boy," the boy continued, and the group cheered again. The woman extended her arm and asked for money. Harley gave her a few rupees, and a few more to the child with the fiery eyes. She started walking away. The woman said something in rapid Hindi. The boy shouted, "Aditi!"

Harley had no idea what this word means. She finished crossing the bridge that led to the ashram. The adventure she had dreamed of was finally underway.

CHAPTER 8

WITH ITS GREEN MOUNTAINS ON one side and the sparkling Ganges River on the other, the ashram projected simplicity and calm. Harley approached the front desk. She introduced herself to a tall young man with brown eyes hidden behind long lashes, curly shoulder-length hair, and a gentle face. He welcomed her with a bashful smile, revealing two dimples.

"Hello," Harley said with a tired smile. "Is there a room available for tonight?"

"Are you alright?" the young man asked and pointed to his forehead, to the same spot where Harley had a large bruise.

Harley had already managed to dismiss the injury she'd suffered on the bus. A small mirror hung on the wall behind the front desk; she stepped over the counter to examine herself. She did not look her best. There was a reddish-purple bruise in the center of her forehead, her hair was matted, and her clothes were wrinkled and damp from bathing in the Ganges.

"Bus accident," she said preemptively.

"I see," said the young man. "Did you leave your luggage at the front door?"

"No, it was a backpack and I lost it," she said, attempting to sound casual.

"I see," he said again, this time with a sympathetic smile.

The room was sparse. It had a single, long narrow window, and the only furniture was a short single bed with a thin mattress. The walls were the same greenish color as the building's exterior, but here, the paint was not peeling, and had turned pink in a few spots, creating delicate flower-like patterns. Harley lay down. Soon her tiredness bested her, and she fell into a deep sleep.

When she woke up, it was already night. Through the small window she saw the black sky and the stars sparkling like glass beads. Feeling better, she left her room for the narrow dark hallway and turned toward the communal showers. After washing her face with cold water, she went back to her room and lay in bed, half-asleep. After some time, Harley heard laughter nearby, followed by the sound of her growling stomach. She got out of bed and considered locking the door until it dawned on her that she had no belongings. Even her small wristwatch had been in the backpack, and she had lost all track of time.

Harley followed the voices up a winding staircase lit with small candles inside niches in the wall. The staircase led to a large balcony on the roof of the ashram. A full moon illuminated the Ganges River in a soft silvery light, and the air was warm and fragrant. Harley was hungry, but when she asked one of the employees if she could order dinner, she was politely told that dinner was already over. She leaned against the balcony rail, trying to take comfort in the magnificent view of the river. Little prayer boxes with candles inside slowly sailed along it, and she recalled how she had bathed in that very place. Then she remembered the odd man and his vague words about golden keys at the bottoms of frozen windswept lakes. Absorbed in thought, she did not notice the young man from the front desk standing in front of her, smiling his bashful smile.

"This isn't your day, is it?"

Harley smiled back.

"I fell asleep and only now woke up," she apologized.

"You must be hungry, no?"

It felt good to have her mind read. "Yes, but I understand I missed dinner."

"I think I can find you something. How about you take a seat here?" the young man offered, pulling back a chair. Harley gratefully acquiesced.

Half an hour later he returned with a tray of perfectly baked nan and vegetables in a light tomato sauce on a bed of basmati rice. Harley could tell it would be the best meal she would eat in India, before even taking a bite.

"I hope I didn't overly trouble the kitchen staff," she said.

"It's fine. In this case the kitchen staff is me," the young man said, and immediately added, "I'm Rajou."

"I'm Harley," she replied.

While she ate with gusto, Rajou sat on one of the nearby chairs and observed the river, stealing furtive glances at the intriguing guest.

Between bites, Harley said, "There's something ancient and mysterious about this river. I can just feel it."

"Yes. We call it Ganga Ma, meaning Mother Ganges, the one who gave life to all of us."

Harley liked the sound of *Ganga Ma* and repeated the words quietly.

"You should see the river during the Kumbh Mela," said Rajou.

"Kumbh *what?*" Harley vaguely remembered the name from one of Shelby's lectures.

"It's a giant festival held every twelve years on the banks of the river. It draws millions of pilgrims and holy people. It's truly a sight to see."

"What's the meaning of *Kumbh Mela?*"

"In Sanskrit, *Kumbh* means 'pitcher.' We believe there was a mighty battle in the sky between gods and demons over a pitcher containing an immortality potion. During the fight, a few drops spilled into the Ganges, right here in Haridwar."

Harley remembered the story from Divya's father.

"And why does the festival happen every twelve years?"

"According to Indian astrology, Jupiter is in Aquarius every twelve years. Kumbh Mela symbolizes the sign of Aquarius, the water bearer pouring knowledge from his pitcher onto the world."

Rajou described how hundreds of holy people living in caves in the Himalayan Mountains covered their naked bodies in dirt and bathed in the Ganges to purify themselves. He told of huge parades of bulls and elephants, fancy canopies, religious rituals, the sound of ancient hymns everywhere, and plays that reenacted what had happened during that fateful battle in the sky. He relayed stories of long moonlit nights full of thousands of candles in small flower baskets sailing along the dark river that promised eternal life to those who believed.

Engrossed by his descriptions, Harley asked, "When is the next festival? Hopefully not in twelve years . . ."

Rajou laughed, displaying his dimples. "No, actually it will take place six months from today."

"Six months . . ." she repeated his words, her voice trailing off. It seemed like an eternity. She wondered how her life would look in six months. Rajou noticed her pensiveness.

"How long are you planning to stay at the ashram?"

"I leave in two days. Do you know where I could buy some clothes and toiletries?"

"That's right!" Rajou slapped his forehead. "You lost your backpack. I am so dense sometimes. All this talking about festivals and ancient tales won't help you change your clothes or freshen up with a decent shower." He burst into a deep and carefree laugh and Harley joined him, charmed by the way he did not take himself too seriously. "There's a small market here where you can get the basics. If you wish, I'll go with you tomorrow morning."

"Sure, great," Harley said, her mood improving by the minute.

"And if you wake up early, you can also make it to a class my dad is teaching."

"Who's your dad?"

"The ashram's owner and senior yoga and meditation instructor. We host people from all over India, and from all over the world."

"Your dad is Babaji?" Harley thought about the letter she'd received from Divya's father but was too embarrassed to admit she had lost it.

"Yes," Rajou replied. "The lesson starts with yoga and meditation and then my father takes some questions from the participants."

"Sounds amazing," Harley said. She was full of thoughts when she returned to her room. From her bed, Harley looked at the full moon lighting up the small room, and as she thought about the long road that awaited her before reaching the ice cave, her eyes grew heavy, and she fell into a deep dreamless sleep.

The next morning, Harley went down to the large lawn and approached a small group of people sitting in a corner. Most of them were foreigners and older than Harley. Babaji was sitting on a raised platform, speaking to the class. When Harley got closer, she saw that his brown eyes were the same as Rajou's.

"You spend your whole lives searching for happiness, but without knowing what it looks like," Babaji said in a soothing voice.

"I think I know," one of the participants said, his long hair falling across his face. Babaji gestured toward him and the young man continued, "To be happy is to know you've accomplished what you set out to do."

Babaji seemed amused by the answer. "Most people want one thing today and, in a few days, desire something else."

The thin man brushed away his hair from his forehead and remained silent.

"It's better to observe a happy person and try to learn how they think and behave," Babaji added.

After a few seconds various people called out: "They laugh a lot." "They're optimistic." "They're calm and patient."

Babaji nodded. "Now we're getting closer to the heart of it. A happy person thinks and behaves a certain way. But you're still missing the most important thing."

"They don't envy others?" a tanned, heavily muscled woman with a butterfly tattoo on her shoulder asked.

"The most important thing," Babaji said, "is attaining inner peace, the kind that is not easily affected by other people's words or actions."

Babaji's words reminded Harley of her conversation with Professor Shelby at the park.

"I've had a few of those moments of inner peace but most of the time I'm stressed," the butterfly woman said.

"That's understandable. It's how most people live their lives. Imagine diving to the depths of an abyss in a vast ocean and finding a rare treasure inside an ancient chest. The problem is that you don't have the key to the chest. You collect a few gold coins scattered around the treasure and return to the surface. Those are the few moments of happiness you are able to experience."

The woman nodded.

"The actual treasure awaits inside that chest," Babaji said with a smile before repeating his earlier words. "But now you must find the key."

He gracefully rose from his seat. Class was over. Harley stood up slowly and began walking out of the ashram. Rajou was waiting for her near a large white boulder. When he saw her, he nodded and smiled his characteristic smile. They walked silently toward the market. A slight fog covered the village laid out before them and the wind was pleasant. Harley's stomach growled as she remembered the dinner Rajou had prepared for her the night before.

"So how did you become such a great cook?"

Rajou seemed to welcome the question. "Ever since I was a kid I loved being in the kitchen with the women and helping them make all sorts of dishes," he explained. "My father always wanted me to follow in his footsteps and become a yoga and meditation teacher, so that I could replace him when the time came for him to retire. I tried following the path he laid out for me for a few years and participated in all classes that were held at the ashram. I even started leading some workshops myself," he said. Then he suddenly fell silent.

"And what happened then?"

"My heart wasn't in it. I want to cook. I love handling the produce and creating new dishes. When I cook, I'm in a different world."

"What does your family think about this passion of yours?"

"The truth is I haven't really talked to them about it yet. They view the time I spend in the kitchen as harmless, a silly experimentation. I'm the only son in my family and they are counting on me to follow in my father's footsteps."

Harley could relate. She knew what it was like to come up against the expectations of a parent pushing their child to excel from a young age.

They arrived at the river. "The market is a few minutes from here," Rajou said. "We can sit here for a bit and talk if you'd like," he pointed toward a wide flat boulder. "I used to sit here for hours as a kid."

They sat on the white boulder, the river flowing below. Around Rajou Harley could be herself, without the need to pretend. Rajou appeared to be comfortable in his own skin, which made her more at ease with herself. Now, as she sat under the caressing sun, listening to the river, she felt a sense of freedom she had never experienced before.

"I understand what you're saying. My mother doesn't really understand what I'm looking for. She tries to help me, but I just can't share with her the whole truth of the path that I'm walking on."

Rajou didn't ask what kind of truth Harley was referring to. Instead, he threw a little pebble into the river and asked, "And what does your father think about your path?"

Harley averted her gaze from him. He looked at her with a curious glance, then picked another pebble and threw it in a long arc into the river. After a few minutes, Rajou continued. "Even if you have been walking down the wrong path for a long time, turn back," he said. "That's an ancient saying I learned from one of the teachers at the ashram."

Harley fingered the pendant around her neck. The key sparkled in the light of the hot sun and Rajou leaned toward it. Harley told him about the jeweler who had made the key at her father's request and engraved her name on it in Sanskrit. Rajou asked her to remove the pendant for a closer look.

"Do you know what's engraved here?"

"I just told you—my name in Sanskrit."

He laughed and crossed his legs. "Is your name Aditi?"

"Aditi?" Harley remembered the old fortune-teller at the bridge and squinted her eyes in confusion.

Rajou smiled softly. "What's engraved here is the name *Aditi*. Aditi is one of our earlier Hindu goddesses. Her name means 'boundless.' I think the jeweler misled your father."

Harley stared at Rajou in amazement. Up until that moment it had never occurred to her to question what her father had told her. She became lost in thought until she realized Rajou was still talking to her.

"Aditi provides protection, success, and bounty to any person who believes in her or carries her name on their body."

"Oh!" Harley snapped out of her reverie. "In that case, I've never been so happy to have been led astray!"

An hour later, on their way back to the ashram, armed with new clothes and supplies, Harley and Rajou were startled by a hoarse shout: "Helllloooooo snake!"

Harley jumped back as an old woman waved a black cobra in front of her. The snake's fanned head was so close that she could see its forked tongue darting in and out of its mouth. Harley took another step back, but the old woman kept accosting her with the snake. Rajou held Harley close and explained that the woman was trying to make a few rupees by letting tourists take pictures with the snake. He told her that she had once possessed healing powers, and that people from all over India came to Haridwar for the potions she brewed, until one day she stopped making them.

When they reached the ashram, Harley was still rattled by the encounter. They went up to the roof and sat on the large balcony. Over warm chai with cinnamon, Harley mustered up the courage to tell Rajou about the journey she was embarking on. Her eyes shone as she described the ice cave from which the great river below them emerged. When she finished talking, she looked up at Rajou and said one last thing: "I am leaving early in the morning. It would be amazing if you came with me to Gangotri and then to the ice cave in the glacier."

Rajou took a long sip of chai, leaned forward, and held Harley's hand without saying a word.

It was dawn. A bird chirped in the distance and a dog let out a long howl. Harley woke up, got dressed, and packed her bag. She went down to the front desk and looked for Rajou. When she saw he was not there, her heart skipped a beat. She paid her bill to a serious looking receptionist, then put on her backpack and took leave of the ashram. As she did so, she prayed that the path she was walking down was not the wrong one Rajou had referred to in the ancient saying. When she passed a crumbling brick wall, her heart skipped a beat again. There was Rajou, sitting on a small boulder, a grey backpack at his feet.

Rajou pointed at the ashram behind them and said, "Last night I told my father about meeting you."

Harley let him continue.

"I told him you invited me to join you. He did not hesitate for a second and said our encounter was no coincidence, and that I should take this journey with you to Gangotri, the most sacred spot in the Himalayas. He said you bring luck and good intentions."

Harley was overjoyed. "It's good to hear I bring good luck. I was beginning to question that." She touched Rajou's shoulder. "Thanks for coming," she said with gleaming eyes.

After arriving at the bridge, which was nearly empty so early in the morning, they walked toward the town's central bus station, where Rajou spoke briefly with a thick-mustached man who shot Harley curious looks.

"He'll take us to Gangotri in his jeep. It's a two-day drive and the price he's asking is reasonable," Rajou translated. The road was narrow and winding, surrounded by green mountains and valleys full of flowers. Harley could not get enough of the view, even from the back seat of the jeep. Below them, the Ganges made its way through a wide valley.

Harley turned to Rajou, "You know, in New York I'm surrounded by giant skyscrapers blocking the sky. Here

I feel utterly at peace with myself, connected to a deep, relaxing place within my body."

"Yes, I get it," Rajou said. "I visited New Delhi a few times and couldn't bear the noise, the crowds, the polluted air. I don't think I'll ever leave this place."

"But don't you dream of discovering new ones?" asked Harley.

He nodded and smiled. "You can read about any place in the world without leaving your home. But you're right, Gangotri is one of the few places I did always want to visit. Reading about it wasn't enough. And now I'm on my way there with you." Reaching for Harley's hand, Rajou clasped it tightly.

They stopped for a light lunch at a teahouse on the side of the road, and after some rice with peppery lentils, continued their way. In the late afternoon they arrived in a town that only had one narrow street. The driver took them to a cheap hostel, and they retired to separate rooms for the night.

Harley tossed and turned on the small bed, wondering about the nature of the connection that was developing between Rajou and her. She knew that he accepted her for who she was, without trying to change her. And there was something else there, a weird feeling that they were simply right for each other, that they were destined to meet. She wondered whether he felt the same way. Then she thought of all that was about to happen to them once they arrived at Gangotri, and of her father's cryptic words about needing to jump into the abyss.

CHAPTER 9

THE JEEP DROVE ALONG a bumpy road. Strong winds began to blow, shaking the treetops. Harley thought about the purpose of this journey. Only on rare occasions did she feel as certain about her choices as she did now, taking this trip in her father's footsteps. She wondered if she could amplify these occasions and boost her confidence about the decisions that awaited her. She turned to Rajou and asked, "Do you think our lives have meaning, or are we just being carried by a random current from one point to the next?"

Rajou stared into the valley, now displayed before them in all its glory, and after a moment said, "I believe questions about the meaning of life are missing the point. If you were to examine your life, you'd discover that what you're really looking for is the experience of feeling alive."

"And how do you get to feel truly alive?" Harley asked, although she was quite sure she was feeling that way right now.

Rajou smiled and held Harley's hand. "I can tell you what works for me. There are a few things that make me look at my life and understand how lucky I am. When I'm in a new place, like here, at the heart of the Himalayas, I feel alive. When I am lying on my back in a sunny green meadow, hearing the birds chirping and the wind on my face, I feel alive. Even when I try creating a new dish with ingredients I haven't used before, I feel alive."

"So really, anything that's new or that makes you connect to yourself brings you closer to that experience?"

"Yes. It's a strange feeling, as if I'm able to take leave of my body and observe what's happening to me from a different perspective. It's me and it's not me. That feeling of 'here I am, at a new place,' or 'here I am, completely calm,' is a wonderful thing."

Harley recalled her experience of bathing in the Ganges the morning after her exhausting night ride. She had felt fully alive there, connected to life and to herself. She looked at Rajou, whose eyes were fixed on the view from the window.

The paved road suddenly ended, and the jeep continued along a narrow dirt road. It was as if they had reached the end of the world, to a place where no vehicles or any other modern trappings were allowed. Rajou seemed transfixed by the view. He did not attempt to start a conversation, which Harley thanked him for in her heart, and his hand remained firmly enclosed in hers. The fact that they could be together without a burning need to fill every moment with words made her feel relaxed around him. It seemed to her that what had begun as an accidental encounter was now turning into something bigger.

The jeep kept toiling up unpaved roads and Harley surrendered to her weariness. Her head hung back, and she fell asleep. When she woke up the jeep was standing still and she was snuggled in the back seat, her head leaning on Rajou's shoulder. Gently touching her hair, Rajou said, "We're here. We've run out of road."

Harley looked out the window. Large white boulders blocked what remained of the road. As they paid the driver, he told them to continue toward the mountains. Harley's stomach was in knots as she gathered her bags. She was finally arriving at the place she had dreamed of.

Gangotri was a small, picturesque town with the Ganges gurgling through it, surrounded by tall rocky cliffs. The few houses in town were alarmingly close to the river, and Harley wondered how safe the residents who lived right above the river felt. The town was situated in a green, blossoming valley, with snowy mountain peaks visible from a distance. Harley and Rajou walked along the town's only street, searching for a small cafe where they could sit and plan their journey together.

There was a white round structure towering at the edge of town that Harley recognized as the temple of the Goddess Ganga, protector of the holy river. Near the temple, a small restaurant overlooked the river and the valley leading to the mountains. Harley bought two bottles of orange juice from a vendor along the way, gave one bottle to Rajou, unscrewed the cap of the other, and drank her fill.

They continued walking along the main street until they saw a sign for another restaurant, near the river. It was nothing more than a few folding tables whose white paint had faded, and some rickety wooden chairs. The only waiter, an older man with a thick mustache, passed by them, carrying a tray with a giant slice of apple pie.

She and Rajou followed him to a raised wooden platform located right above the raging river. Bottle of juice in hand, Harley moved carefully toward the platform. They gingerly stepped on it, the river rapidly flowing beneath them. In addition to them, there was one other customer, facing the opposite direction and feverishly writing in a journal bound in leather. A half-eaten piece of apple pie rested on his table beside a cup of tea.

Placing the fresh pie on the diner's table, the waiter cleared the half-eaten piece. When the customer turned his head to thank him, the bottle of juice fell from Harley's hand and shattered onto the wooden platform. The man with the journal was none other than Dr. Mark Shelby! Harley froze in place, while Shelby smiled as if this chance meeting in the Himalayas had been just what he was expecting.

He got up from his seat, stepped over the glass, shook pie crumbs off his pants, and extended a hand to Rajou.

"Mark Shelby, nice to meet you," he addressed the young man with a generous smile.

"Rajou," the young man replied.

At record speed, the waiter appeared with a broom and dustpan and began collecting the glass shards. Harley observed him as if hypnotized, noticing the flexibility and coordination of his movements, none of them superfluous. A minute later the platform was clean again.

Shelby noticed the bruise on Harley's forehead. "What happened to you?" he asked with concern.

Harley tried to speak, but her voice betrayed her.

Shelby smiled understandingly. "I see you are surprised by my sudden appearance here."

"That's an understatement," she managed to say.

"Our conversations must have gotten to me," the professor mused. "I came to hike along the same track I lecture about at the university."

"You lecture at a university?" Rajou asked in awe.

"Yes, and Harley is one of my best students," the professor said, winking at Harley.

Harley did not respond. There was something different about Shelby, an astounding vitality he had lacked in New York. Her professor seemed reborn. It was as if he had shed his old skin and arrived in India younger and bursting with fresh energy. Gesturing to two available seats near his table, he said, "Why don't you join me for tea and some delicious apple pie?"

Rajou smiled and said, "I saw you didn't finish the first slice. Are you sure the pie is delicious?"

Shelby laughed and said, "You're perceptive. Indeed, the first slice wasn't that great, and that's why I ordered a second one."

"Don't you think you'll get exactly the same thing?"

"You never know what you'll get when you ask for something a second time. The waiter saw I didn't finish the first slice. There's always a chance they have another pie in the back and that the second time may be different." Shelby sat down, took a bite with his fork, and said, "Totally different."

Rajou smiled. "I'd never think to order the same thing if I was disappointed the first time."

"It's one of the tricks I learned over the course of my travels," Shelby explained. "Most people don't give the other party a chance to improve. At the end of the day, we all figure things out by trial and error."

"My dad always told me that until I try things for myself, I'll never truly learn anything," Rajou said.

"And he's right," Professor Shelby agreed. "Now come, sit with me, and try the new pie."

Rajou and Harley took to the tall chairs, Harley sneaking a sidelong glance at Professor Shelby, trying to piece together the puzzle laid out before her. Dismissing her stare, Shelby ordered tea and pie for his young guests. "This place is fascinating. See that temple over there?" he asked, pointing at the white temple at the edge of town.

"That's where the pilgrims end their long journey that sometimes lasts several months, and present their offerings to the Goddess Ganga, the protector of this magnificent river."

"It's lucky we're here this season. In winter, the snow blocks all access to the town, and you can't come here," Rajou said. He turned to Harley. "Your professor knows many things."

When the apple pie arrived, Harley tasted hers. It was impossibly sweet. Rajou took a bite and made a face. "Wow," he said.

"You should have tried the first piece," Shelby said. "It was even sweeter. At any rate, you're going to need all that sugar for the journey to the glacier."

"How do you know we're planning to go to the glacier?" Rajou asked.

"If I remember correctly," Shelby glanced at Harley, "that ice cave, the source of the Ganges, is the one that sparked our adventurous friend's imagination during my lecture."

Harley remained silent. She was angry at herself for sharing her plans with Professor Shelby, and at him for barging into her dream without an invitation.

Rajou turned to Shelby and asked, "Are you also hoping to make it to the ice cave?"

"Yes," he replied. "I would very much like to go there."

"What do you say the three of us go on this journey together?" Rajou asked Harley.

She looked at the two of them. Something about Professor Shelby's unexpected appearance in such a remote place did not add up. An inner voice told her not to trust him, that there was some hidden reason for his arrival in Gangotri, at the edge of the world, at this exact moment. But then she reminded herself that she too was hiding secrets, and that there was no valid reason for her to refuse to add him to the adventure.

"Sure, why not, sounds like a good idea."

Shelby and Rajou both smiled at her.

Pulling a large map out of his backpack, Shelby spread it on the table, and he and Rajou began a lively discussion about the gear they would need, how long it would take them to reach the glacier, and where they should sleep along the way. The river kept flowing amidst smooth giant rocks, and soon the sun began to disappear. As it did so, it cast the stone walls around them in a golden light. At nightfall, Shelby suggested they stay in the small hotel that he had checked into, and Harley and Rajou accepted his invitation.

The next morning, after purchasing their supplies, they began walking toward the small temple in Gangotri. The mighty Himalayan Mountains watched over them in graceful silence, concealing countless secrets and adventures and inviting the newly formed trio to join the other explorers who had walked the same path for generations.

CHAPTER 10

HARLEY BELIEVED SHE HAD MADE peace with Shelby's unexpected appearance by the time they passed by Gangotri's ancient temple and entered a wide valley. The sun shone happily on them. They were now a unified group of three on their way to the glacier. At least this was what Harley kept trying to tell herself. Rajou and Shelby began a lively discussion about pilgrimages to the Himalayas and Harley felt for a moment that she was traveling back in time to Columbia University, to the lecture that would alter her world. The only difference was that now she was on her way to the glacier herself, instead of merely reading about it in a book. The blossoming valley looked to her like a dream come true, the air was outrageously clear, and every so often Himalayan blue sheep appeared on the distant mountain slopes.

Rajou turned to Shelby. "How does it feel to actually be here instead of lecturing about it in class?"

"There's no substitute for reality," Shelby said, smiling. He glanced at Harley and said, "I feel like I am at the start of an adventure toward the unknown."

Harley thought of how good it would feel to be free of all the secrets and lies that hung above her like a dark cloud. She had not shared her reason for being here with anyone but Divya. For a moment she considered telling her two travel companions the truth but decided this was not the right time or place.

They stopped for lunch at an improvised tea hut on the side of the road. The young vendor was accompanied by his wife, and two small children bashfully peeked out from behind their mother's apron. Sitting on the ground, they enjoyed a rice stew with vegetables. Shelby was the first to finish his meal. He leaned back against a tree, sipped from his water bottle, took out his leather journal, and began writing diligently.

"May I ask what you're writing about?" Harley asked.

He kept writing for a moment and then paused and looked up at her. "I'm writing about what I see and experience here. One day it may prove valuable."

Rajou nodded, as if he had just been offered a rare pearl of wisdom. Harley could not help but roll her eyes. She noticed that Rajou regarded Shelby with boundless respect and for some reason this bothered her. *No one is perfect*, she thought to herself: I am hiding my real reason for making this journey, Rajou refuses to confront his family, and Shelby is not forthcoming. He's shrouded in a mystery whose source I can't figure out.

An hour later they got up, thanked the vendor, and started walking again. After several hours they arrived at an abandoned hut overlooking the flowing river below. The hut was dusty, the chipped wooden floor was black with dirt, and drafts of cold air came in from a large hole in the ceiling. They spread their sleeping bags on the floor and silently looked at the stars visible through the hole. Harley lay in her sleeping bag and thought of how far she was from the safe life she was used to. The three quickly fell asleep, tired from the first day of their journey and its exhausting physical demands.

By morning, the water in their canteens was nearly frozen. They boiled water on a small camping burner they had brought along and had tea and biscuits. After this modest breakfast, they continued walking along the path. Rajou and Shelby walked in front of Harley. Shelby said something to Rajou and they both started laughing. There was an easy camaraderie between them, a natural connection.

Rajou turned to Shelby and asked, "What's the most important thing you learned throughout your years of exploring Eastern religions?"

Shelby pondered the question for a moment, and then said, "The Buddha said it two thousand years ago: We must recognize that a great deal of suffering and pain exist in the world."

Rajou nodded in agreement. Harley, on the other hand, thought that Shelby had provided a conveniently vague answer.

"That doesn't sound particularly encouraging," she said.

"True," Shelby said. "But that is just a starting point to explain the source of suffering."

"What *is* the source of suffering?" Harley asked.

"Holding onto things," Professor Shelby said.

"Holding onto things? That could mean so many things," Harley said. "You mean we shouldn't grow attached to material things, like our physical possessions?"

"Yes, but not just that. To our emotions, as well."

"But how can we part from our emotions? Why would we?"

Rajou stepped into the conversation. "My dad would say you have to learn to control your negative emotions. If, for example, you feel envy, you mustn't jump and ride that beast. You have to look it in the eye and send it back where it came from."

Harley considered what he was saying. She didn't want to dismiss Rajou, or even Shelby, but their ideas seemed overly simplistic. "This seems like an impossible task to me. I know it's destructive to be envious of other people, but this sounds like a futile struggle."

Shelby said, "No one expects you to get rid of all of your negative emotions overnight. Begin today and always keep practicing. You have your whole life ahead of you. When you're ready, you'll be able to send that beast on its way," he said and affectionately tapped Rajou's shoulder.

Rajou was overjoyed that the professor had endorsed his expression. Harley silently contemplated Shelby's words, and as the three walked by a stream, Rajou turned to her and said,

"It took me a long time to learn how to fight my negative emotions. I was lucky to have excellent teachers and to start at a young age."

"You never feel jealousy or other negative emotions?" Harley asked, amazed.

"I struggle with those feelings the same way you do. I've just been doing this for several years now, that's the only difference."

Harley said, "I missed that train."

Shelby sent her a quick look and said with a smile, "It would have been best to begin this struggle with jealousy and other negative emotions a long time ago. The second-best option is to begin today—right here and now."

Shelby spoke with a smile, but behind it was a lot of power and conviction. Harley was impressed with the way he delivered this message. She looked at Shelby and said, "I still don't understand what exactly I should do when I feel envy or anger."

"The first step is awareness," Shelby told her. "Understanding that negative feelings have no value, that they add nothing to your life, would be great progress." As they kept on walking, he added quietly, "All they do is making your precious dreams become smaller and insignificant."

"What do you mean"? asked Harley.

"If, for example, you are jealous of a friend who has a lot of money, you're going to tell yourself that she became rich by ill gains, or by unethical behavior, or by sacrificing her personal life. The result is the same—you will rob yourself of the opportunity to become rich yourself."

Harley thought about what Shelby had just said and realized that he was right. Comparing herself to others and belittling their achievements was pointless. It would not help her achieve anything. She turned to Shelby and said, "I'm getting the impression that fighting these negative emotions is a tall order."

He nodded in agreement and replied, "Think of it as a long, dangerous war, one where you will do anything to survive. This is the mindset you need to adopt. Anytime you have a negative emotion you must fight it using your life force, your entire being. Stop everything else and focus all your energy on not expressing the feeling. You can't be complacent. These emotions are like toxins and if you let them stay in your body, they will literally poison you."

Harley wondered again about the powerful conviction that was behind Shelby's words. It seemed like this was something he paid a lot of attention to. Perhaps he had struggled with it himself for a long time.

The road curved upward. Rajou turned to Shelby and said, "What you're saying is whenever we are about to express a negative emotion, we should fight the urge with everything we've got."

Shelby patted Rajou's shoulder affectionately and said, "Exactly, Rajou. That's exactly what you have to do."

They kept walking the mountain trail. On one of the bends, they encountered a pilgrim who had turned around midway to the glacier and was on his way back. He seemed about sixty, tall and slender. He wore a thin white tunic with a vest on top, and his toes peeked out from his sandals. He looked ridiculously unprepared to travel on foot across snowy mountains, but he did not seem to suffer from the cold. The pilgrim smiled and greeted them. They greeted him back and Rajou invited him to sit with them and share their snack of apples, which they had bought in Gangotri. Rajou conversed with the pilgrim for a while, and after a few minutes turned to Shelby and Harley and said, "Looks like we can't climb the glacier. A blizzard has been raging there for several days."

Harley and Shelby exchanged disappointed looks. Harley looked up toward the top of the mountain, thinking about everything she'd had to do to get there. Shelby reached out and touched her shoulder. "Hey, all is not lost. You never know what the weather is going to be like once we reach high altitude. We might still make it." She smiled ruefully, nodded her head, and said nothing. The pilgrim watched this exchange with rapt attention, then said a few things to Rajou, which Rajou translated for his friends.

"The man says he's happy. Even though he failed to achieve his goal of reaching the source of the Ganges, he managed to receive the blessing of a holy man, what we call a swami, who lives in a cave about two hours from here."

Rajou's eyes shone with excitement. He continued, "He says that the swami doesn't accept many visitors. If your heart is pure and your intentions are noble, he'll agree to receive you."

Harley wondered if they measured up to the swami's standards. Rajou took out a notebook from his backpack and the man quickly jotted down a few landmarks in it.

"We have to search for a big boulder in a river that looks like a teardrop," Rajou explained. "The swami's cave is high in the mountain above that boulder."

With his walking stick, Shelby tapped on a white boulder to his left. "We're wasting valuable time," he determined. "We should continue walking toward the glacier."

They said goodbye to the pilgrim. Harley and the professor walked at a slow pace, each thinking about how they might have come all this way only to return without reaching their destination. Rajou felt the tension in the air and began singing a song to himself with a compelling rhythm. The words swirled around them, and after a few minutes Harley asked what the song was about. He told them it was an ancient song about seekers embarking on a long journey. In his family, this song had been passed down from generation to generation. He translated the first verse for Harley:

> like a warm breeze
> in a snowy desert
> keep dreaming
> my brothers and sisters
> keep dreaming

Harley smiled. She regained her strength. The lyrics penetrated straight through her heart and the ancient message in the old song cheered her up and lifted her spirit. "I can't stop dreaming," she told herself. "I have to keep believing."

She was determined to make it to the glacier.

CHAPTER 11

AFTER PASSING ANOTHER BEND IN the road, they saw the big teardrop-shaped boulder at the center of the river.

"Let's look for the cave!" Harley called out.

"We should keep walking," Professor Shelby said. He looked toward the mountains. Grey clouds were gathering above the snowy summit. "The weather is unstable; it's best we continue walking."

"But we're already here," Harley said. "Who knows if we'll ever return to this place?"

Rajou nodded in agreement. "To receive a blessing from such a holy man is no small matter," he said earnestly.

Shelby shot them both a stern look. "Don't you understand the risk we're taking by getting delayed here?" He pointed toward the distant, foggy mountains. "I say we continue toward the glacier. We can try looking for this obscure cave on our way back."

Shelby set out along the path.

"Wait!" Rajou called out. "It's more important to receive the swami's blessing now, before we attempt to reach the glacier and the ice cave."

Harley called to Shelby, "Rajou is right. Let's spend the next hour looking for the cave. If we find it, we'll receive the blessing and continue our way. If we don't, at least we'll know we tried."

With Shelby back on board, Rajou pointed to a narrow pathway above them leading to the top of the canyon. They began the climb. The trail was winding and precarious. Loose rocks littered the path, adding uncertainty to each step. With no cave in sight, Harley wondered how one could live here, alone, in the heart of the mountains. They were about to turn back when suddenly, far above them, Rajou noticed a glimmer of light refracting on the boulders. After another strenuous ascent they spotted the entrance to a cave inside the mountain. When they reached the cave, they saw that the glimmer of light had been coming from a rusty metal bucket filled with clean water.

The cave was long, narrow, and dark. Candles flickered in a few nooks, throwing quivering shadows onto the walls. Near the entrance they beheld a white-bearded man wrapped in orange clothes sitting on a mat, his eyes closed. It was difficult to determine his age, but there was a timelessness to him. Without a word, he slowly opened his calm black eyes, which came to rest on each of them. Harley noticed him smiling to himself as he peacefully examined them. He did not seem at all surprised by these unexpected visitors. Rising from his place with remarkable flexibility, he greeted them in Hindi. Rajou bowed his head; Harley and Shelby followed suit.

Later they sat outside the cave and drank tea prepared by the swami. Shelby and Rajou spread out maps and planned the rest of the trip. The next stop was at a place called Bhojbasa, a small cluster of huts at the foot of the glacier. From there, weather permitting, they would go straight to the source of the Ganges.

Time passed slowly. The sun had long set. Shelby suggested they continue on their way, but the swami insisted they stay for the night as his guests and leave in the morning. They spent the rest of the evening in silence, each ensconced in their sleeping bag. From inside hers, Harley studied the narrow cave. She could see no source of light, but outside the sky was black and full of sparkling stars. She felt lucky to be in such a special place and debated going to the cave's entrance to observe the stars. But the physical effort she had exerted during the day got the best of her, and she quickly fell asleep.

In the morning, the swami made them tea, accompanied by biscuits. As they ate, he headed to the side of the cave, opened a large wooden chest, and began rummaging through it. He took out a few old photo albums and handed them to Rajou, who translated, "These are photo albums of the area and the glacier. The swami says many travelers send him photos and he keep them in these albums." Rajou handed one album to Harley and another to Shelby.

Harley began flipping through the pages. She saw photos of the swami as a young man, in all sorts of complicated yoga poses. Placing the album in front of the swami, she pointed to a photo of him in an especially tricky one. The swami glowed, and to Harley's amazement, recreated the pose. His flexibility was remarkable, and Harley laughed in awe at a man so old displaying such strength and poise.

Rajou and Shelby smiled at the swami and went back to examining the map. A cold wind penetrated the cave, causing Harley to tighten the collar of her coat. Turning to another photo, she suddenly gasped as the image of a man came into focus. He was standing outside the swami's cave, his arm around the shoulder of another man. Both men were laughing and appeared healthy and strong. Harley held the album closer to her face, overtaken by longing and grief.

The picture was of none other than her father.

Observing her distress, the swami said something, but she didn't hear him. She was preoccupied with examining the man standing next to her father in the photo. He had a bushy pile of hair covering half his face, but something was disturbingly familiar about him. As she slowly put down the album, she tried to recall how she might have met him.

The swami picked up the album, opened it to the photo of her father, and said something in Hindi, addressed to Professor Shelby. Rajou translated, "I still remember what happened to your friend." His voice shook as he spoke the rest of the swami's words, "I'm glad you brought your daughter here."

Shelby did not dare look at Harley, and Rajou had become as pale as a ghost. As Harley examined the man with his arm around her father again, it hit her like a punch to the gut. Right before her father had disappeared, Shelby had been with him in this very cave, and now the swami was mistaking her for Shelby's daughter. The repercussions of this discovery overwhelmed her. She stood up and with quivering legs began to exit the cave. Shelby tried to stop her, but she pushed his arm away, broke free, and began running down a steep slope.

Shelby and Rajou were right behind her. "Harley, wait! I can explain everything!" Shelby called out.

She ignored him and continued downward.

"Harley! Let me explain!"

Without stopping, Harley looked back and yelled, "I don't want to speak to you ever again! You knew this whole time . . ."

Losing her footing, Harley slipped and began rolling down the slope. Rajou tried to catch her, but to no avail. A moment later, her head hit a large boulder.

CHAPTER 12

HARLEY LAY AT THE BOTTOM of the slope. Rajou and Shelby picked her up and carefully placed her under a broad-leafed alder tree, splashing cold water on her face. Her head was pounding and the pain in her ribs was sharp. First, she saw Rajou hovering above her and then Shelby, a concerned look on his face. Unable to bear the sight of him, she looked away.

"You must have a guardian angel," Rajou said, and encouraged Harley to rest.

A light snow began to fall. After some time, Harley's pain started to subside, and she got up to sit on a jagged rock, close to the river. She recalled the meeting in Professor Shelby's office, and his warnings about the dangers of embarking on such a journey. Now she understood why he had tried to stop her. It was maddening to realize she had come to him for guidance, only for him to lie and give her advice that suited his own agenda—an agenda he had told her nothing about. After several minutes of sitting utterly still, Harley cupped icy water in her hands and splashed it onto her face.

A new thought occurred to her—Shelby had been the last person to see her father alive. He knew what had happened to him. Some old hope that her father was still alive reawakened in her. No one had found his body and he'd been declared dead a month after he disappeared. Perhaps Shelby knew something the others didn't? A new thought replaced the old one, sending a chill down Harley's aching spine—perhaps Shelby was responsible for her father's death and that's why he'd never told anyone what happened. Was it possible he had come here to keep the truth out of her reach? Either way, Shelby knew her father's fate, and Harley did not.

Her thoughts swirling, Harley saw Professor Shelby coming down the slope. When he reached her, he sat down next to her on the jagged rock. Harley did not move. Neither of them spoke. After several silent minutes Shelby reached into his shirt pocket and pulled out the photo of her father and him. "I miss him so much," he said quietly, as if speaking to himself. "It causes me actual physical pain."

Harley glanced at the stranger sitting next to her. He suddenly looked several years older—tired and confused.

Shelby put the photo back in his pocket. "They say time heals everything, every ache and wound," he said without conviction. Turning his gaze to the river in front of them, he continued, "It's true. Time does dull most pains, but I still find myself dealing with the same sense of loss I felt eight years ago, here in Gangotri." Meeting Harley's eyes for a moment, he added, "I suppose your mother is in the same situation."

At these unexpected words, Harley tensed. "What exactly do you know about my mother?" she asked.

Shelby looked relieved by the question, as if it were long overdue. "We went to college together in California, the three of us. That you already know," he said. "Your father and I were madly in love with your mother, but Jack was the one who won her over. I didn't stand a chance against him."

Harley was shocked by this revelation. It wasn't just Shelby—her mother had been hiding things as well, keeping her own daughter in the dark.

"I met with Sarah in New York as soon as I returned from India," Shelby went on. "I told her what happened." He lowered his gaze before adding, "And then she severed all ties with me."

Harley was at a loss of words. All these years she had been treated like a child. Her mother had not told her the whole truth, while her professor, the best friend she never knew her father had, had gone along with the charade. No longer could she tiptoe around what she deserved to know. It was now or never.

"I want to know what really happened to my dad," Harley demanded.

"Jack was remarkably persuasive," Shelby said in almost dreamlike state. "He called me from Rishikesh and told me about this journey to the source of the Ganges. He said this adventure would change our lives. Ten days later I was here with him, with all the gear we had bought . . ."

Harley cut him off. "What happened to him?"

"You know what happened. You lost your father, and I lost my best friend," he said in a low voice.

Harley wanted to continue asking about the circumstances of her father's death, but strangely enough, now that she was so close to the truth, she was suddenly scared to learn it. Besides, the vacant expression on Shelby's face told her there was nothing more she could get him to say. Looking depleted, Shelby stood up. "I'm sorry. For everything," he said simply to Harley, then headed back to the cave.

It was getting dark. Harley had not eaten, nor had she had anything to drink since her small breakfast. When she stood up, she felt dizzy and grabbed a tree branch for support. She heard footsteps behind her and saw Rajou crossing the river, skipping over the smooth rocks with ease. A moment later, his long arms were warmly embracing her, and his soft lips were seeking hers. Harley felt her anger and confusion dissipate. She returned Rajou's embrace, then let him lead her back up toward the cave. When they arrived, they saw the swami and Shelby outside, sitting cross-legged, quietly observing the mighty mountains surrounding them.

Harley and Rajou entered the cave, while Shelby helped the swami light a fire before joining the others inside. As night fell and the cold set in, the swami sat outside, his legs folded in meditation. Inside the cave, candles cast eerie shadows across the three silent figures wrapped in blankets. Eventually, Harley stood up to go sit next to the swami. His eyes were closed, his face calm, and he did not appear to be breathing. Harley had never tried meditating before, but as she inhaled deeply, she felt her mind begin to clear.

The night was full of stars. Harley felt they were in a distant and mysterious place with unfamiliar rules. The canyon walls around her rose to infinity. *This looks like the edge of the world*, she thought to herself. Even though they were amid the world's tallest mountains, the giant rock walls closing in on them and the complete quiet made her think of the silence at the very bottom of the ocean, where no person had ever walked before.

Closing her eyes, Harley summoned the sensation from an underwater abyss. The water around her was thick and black but somehow pleasant. She took a deep breath, and her entire body relaxed. In such a place, no one could ever reach her; there was no movement or even any source of light—just the peaceful feeling of the water around her. Her breathing slowed and a slight smile fluttered across her lips.

After a while Harley felt a thought trying to catch her, like a puppy nipping at her heels. Focusing on it, she saw herself sitting on the riverbank and playing with the flowing water after having discovered Shelby was with her father in his final moments. She looked at the girl in the picture and sensed her sadness, her loneliness, her anger. After a while, the picture blurred. Harley stayed in the underwater abyss until a voice inside her told her it was time to return to the surface. She began swimming upward, carried by a warm current.

When she opened her eyes, Harley saw that the fire had gone out. The swami was still sitting there, motionless, a thin smile across his face. Harley realized she had probably been in this calm state for no more than a few minutes, yet she'd still managed to experience an illuminating quiet. Inside the cave, Shelby was tossing and turning in his sleeping bag. Harley was surprised to discover the sight of him no longer made her angry, despite having every reason to resent him. From her own sleeping bag, she soon fell into a dreamless sleep.

When she woke up in the morning, Harley was alone in the cave. She got up, stretched, and went outside. Rajou was busy baking thin pitas over an improvised fire and when he saw her, his face lit up. Harley was enamored by the new intimacy between them, especially now, when she needed a friend more than ever. Rajou skillfully removed the thin dough from a round metal lid on top of the fire, topped the dough with a fragrant wedge of cheese, and turned to Harley. "This chapati is the best I can do under these conditions," he said, offering her a taste. "How are you feeling?"

"Better," Harley replied, eating hungrily. "Luckily for me it wasn't a serious blow." Softly, she added, "Thanks for being with me yesterday."

Rajou nodded. "You experienced quite a few things."

"Yes," Harley agreed. She looked at the fog covering the snowy valley. Small clouds surrounded them, and the thick fog twisted like a large snake between the mighty peaks.

"Shelby went down to the river at dawn," Rajou said. "He hasn't spoken to us since what happened yesterday."

"I know I haven't been honest with you until now about my father and the purpose of this journey of mine," she said. "I am sorry. Turned out that this cave exposed my secret as well as Shelby's."

Rajou placed his hand on Harley's shoulder. "I understand why you had a hard time being candid at first. Don't you worry about me. How do you feel about what you have learned about Shelby and your father?"

"I don't know," Harley replied. "Yesterday I was angry and confused. Today I just want to know what happened and why Shelby never said anything all these years."

"Do you think your mother knew any of this?"

"More than she ever let on." Thinking about all that had been hidden from her still hurt her deeply, but Harley tried not to dwell on it. She was here now, and her mother was not.

Harley told Rajou about her meditation in the presence of the swami, and her experience in the underwater abyss. After she finished, Rajou turned to the swami and began speaking to him. For a few minutes, the swami merely looked toward the mountains, and said nothing. Then, like the water from the riverbank below, his words began to flow. "You are on a spiritual journey," Rajou translated. "What's important for you to know is that your father is here with you now and that . . ."

Harley interrupted. "Tell him that Shelby is not my father. My father is the man in the picture who disappeared eight years ago!"

Rajou translated her words and the swami turned to speak directly to Harley. "Your father is here with you now," he repeated. "You must protect him just as he must protect you. Your destinies are intertwined," the swami said, pressing the palms of his hands together, "like two sides of a conch that are forever stuck together."

The swami's words were a bitter pill for Harley to swallow, perhaps because they rang so true. The thought that Shelby had an important role in her life, now that her father was gone, troubled her. But then she saw the image she had tried to dispel the previous night, that of the sad angry girl by the water. She knew she did not want to be that girl any longer. Harley waited for the swami to continue, but he had returned to looking silently at the clouds moving swiftly across the gorge.

CHAPTER 13

RAJOU POINTED TOWARD THE DARK sky in the distance and said, "This does not look good."

"Yes," the swami agreed. "And it is only the beginning." He went back inside the cave, lit another candle, and sat on his mat with his legs crossed and his eyes closed.

When Shelby returned to the cave, Harley was relieved to see him and realized that strangely enough, the old swami was right. There was indeed a mysterious, powerful bond between Shelby and her. She stood up and approached him.

"I've been thinking about what happened yesterday," she said. "I sense that you've been hiding what happened to my father to protect me in some way. I still don't exactly understand why, but I can tell his death hurts you just as much as it hurts me."

Now Shelby looked relieved himself. "I thought you had already suffered enough and that perhaps I could spare you more pain," he said.

"Would you like a cup of tea?" Harley pointed to the pot Rajou had made that morning.

"I'd love one," Shelby said, rubbing his arms vigorously.

Over their steaming mugs, Harley turned to Shelby and asked, "What do you think my father would have said about this adventure of mine?"

"I think he would have said you are impatient," he replied and let out a chuckle. "What's interesting is that your father always spoke about the importance of patience, but when we worked together, I discovered that he himself was not a very patient man."

Harley smiled, recalling the time that her father had taken her out of school in the middle of the day to go sledding. "You worked together?"

"Indeed," Shelby said. "Remember what I told you about the personal growth theory, and the group that developed it?"

Harley thought back to the conversation in the park in New York and how it had ended the moment she'd asked Shelby about the group's members.

As if reading her mind, Shelby looked Harley straight in the eye and said, "Your mother was the third member of our group. She actually managed the whole research and writing process; your father and I would not have gotten any work done if it hadn't been for her."

Harley shook her head in disbelief.

"After Jack disappeared, your mother halted all of our research. I think we both felt we could no longer work together, so we decided to simply drop the entire matter."

Harley found her tongue again. "And how did you all end up working together in the first place?" she asked.

"Your parents roped me in. Their focus back then was developmental psychology, the study of how people change over the course of a lifetime. Most psychologists believe that you don't change after you reach the age of thirty. We felt that this was a short-sighted view, that people can experience significant growth throughout their lives."

Harley was intrigued. "Go on."

"Some people indeed stop developing in early adulthood. They gain life experiences, but they see the world the same way. And then there are those who continue to grow—to have a purpose in each stage of their life."

"What kind of purpose are your referring to?"

"Overcoming your own fears; helping others achieve their goals; ultimately becoming the person you were meant to be."

"And what happens to those who don't change?" Harley asked. Shelby didn't answer right away. He stared at the river below for some time and then said, "Take water, for example," pointing to the river below. "River water is always changing. It can be murky above muddy soil, slow while flowing in a winding channel, or clear right before it merges with the ocean. Now think about standing water. In no time at all it becomes stale and moldy, undrinkable."

"You must move forward all the time?" Harley asked, nodding her head.

"That's right. When we interviewed people who lived their life that way, with forward momentum, not afraid of life's changes but embracing and preparing for them, we found a remarkable pattern. We called it the Principle of Eighteen."

Harley remembered their conversation in New York about the importance of the number eighteen in different cultures, and how Shelby had suggested she use that number throughout her life.

"Hold that thought," Harley said, and went to refill the teapot.

When she returned, Shelby lifted his tea toward Harley's, and they clinked mugs as if in celebration. Then he picked up where he'd left off: "What we discovered is that people who managed to live a full and successful life went through five life stages, from birth to old age. We couldn't believe it when we saw that the stages were pretty much of equal length."

"What do you mean?"

"Every eighteen years or so you need to go through a new stage, a fresh start. The first stage is the Dreamer, where the goal is to conjure a powerful vision for your future self, a dream so compelling that you can't stop thinking about it. Next is the Explorer, which takes place from age eighteen to thirty-six. This is where you seek out your life's calling, that which makes you genuinely happy. At age thirty-six the Builder stage begins. This is where you set up a solid foundation for your future. In your fifties you are in the Mentor stage, sharing your life lessons with younger generations. And finally, in our seventies comes the Giver stage, when you dedicate yourself to a cause that is near and dear to your heart."

Harley nodded, trying to keep up. "How do you make the most out of each stage without getting stuck in it?" she asked.

"That's the key," Shelby said, holding up a finger for emphasis. "Some people settle too soon for what life has to offer them. They hold onto what's safe and familiar exactly at the stage where they should be more daring, exploring what they are capable of and what they could accomplish with their lives."

"Can you give me an example?"

"Take, for example, a young woman, in her early twenties, trying to achieve the promise of the Builder stage instead of pursuing something that genuinely interests her. Maybe she'll go to law school, simply because it sounds prestigious, or she'll start a business without knowing the first thing about managing one."

"Looks like timing plays a big part here," said Harley.

"That's right. Being in the Dreamer stage your whole life is also not a good thing. And same with the Explorer stage. You have eighteen years to explore different paths.

The goal is to find out the one thing that you are passionate about and can be exceptional at."

Harley glanced sympathetically at Shelby. "Do you mean to tell me older people don't explore and take risks?"

Shelby laughed. "Look where I am right now. Deep in the Indian Himalayas. And I have no idea how this adventure will end."

Just then Rajou and the swami appeared and quietly sat next to them. Like a seasoned student, Harley explained to Rajou the main points of Shelby's model. He listened intently and translated for the swami, who replied in a few succinct sentences. Rajou translated his words:

"The number eighteen is a magical number in the Hindu tradition. You can understand many things by using this number. The Bhagavad Gita, our holy scripture, is eighteen chapters long, as is the first Veda, our earliest holy scripture, protected by Lord Brahma himself."

Shelby turned to Rajou. "However you choose to live your life, remember that everything in the universe is constantly changing, growing, dying, and being reborn," he said. "Even the Bible tells us that 'for everything there is a season, and a time for every purpose under heaven.' More importantly, it warns that 'whatsoever a man soweth, that shall he also reap.' Too many of us get that wrong, by starting to reap before we have sown the seeds of our harvest."

"And what happens if I keep dreaming after I'm eighteen?" asked Rajou.

"Then you'll probably sleep well at night," Shelby said with a broad smile and patted Rajou on the back.

Before returning to the cave to pack up their belongings, the swami turned to Rajou, placed his hand on top of his head, and blessed him. Rajou bowed in gratitude. Next was a blessing for Harley: "You have the strength to change yourself."

Harley bowed her head and kissed the swami's hand.

Finally, the swami turned to Shelby. "May you find the joy we all deserve in life," he wished him with a smile.

As they walked toward the mouth of the cave, the swami uttered a few final words, which Rajou translated:

> Remove the masks
> face the truth
> love will rise up
> like a cork at the bottom
> of a deep, dark ocean.

CHAPTER 14

THEY HEADED DOWN FROM THE cave toward a path that led them deep into the heart of the mountains. Shelby was in front, Harley right behind him, and Rajou behind her. The sky was metallic grey, and a cold wind had begun to blow. After walking quietly for a while, Shelby looked back at Harley.

"Are you in touch with Charlie?" he asked.

"Yes," she replied, and left it at that.

"I know he put a lot of effort into searching for Jack."

"How come you never told him?"

Shelby thought for a moment, then said, "Once you start hiding something, there is only a small window during which the truth can come out. Afterward the lie becomes hard and impenetrable, like a fossil."

Harley thought that Charlie would have been happy to learn the truth at any time, even after all these years. Shelby picked up his pace and after a few minutes Harley stopped trying to keep up with him. Rajou and Harley were now walking side by side. Harley took his hand and held it.

"Thanks for everything you've done for me," she said.

"There's nothing you need to thank me for," Rajou said, holding Harley's hand tightly.

"Well, then at least for that breakfast you made. Just thinking about it makes my mouth water."

Rajou smiled. "Chapati hardly counts as breakfast." Kicking a small rock in his path, he said, "You know, I too have been thinking about what I want to do with my life. I don't want to give up on my dream of becoming a chef. My family is counting on me to keep running the ashram after my father retires, but that's their dream, not mine."

"You will make a wonderful chef," Harley said. He squeezed her hand and said nothing. They continued walking until they saw that Shelby was waiting for them near a large boulder, his hand pointing at the black storm clouds converging on the snowy mountain peaks.

"The clouds look so far away, don't they?" Shelby said. "But they're not. We're in a place so high and remote that the basic rules of weather don't apply. Everything can change in an instant."

Adjusting his backpack, Shelby began walking at a brisk pace. Harley and Rajou followed.

Harley called out to him, "Do you really think those clouds could reach us?"

"The mountains teach excellent life lessons. They quickly reveal who's willing to take risks, who's afraid of their own shadow, and who is thinking only of themselves." With his walking stick, Shelby steered away from a steep slope. "But the mountains are not a forgiving teacher. They rarely give one a second chance."

The black clouds began encroaching on larger sections of sky. Snow blanketed the entire valley in a velvety white. Without thinking, Harley pushed Rajou playfully into a pile of fresh snow. Happily surprised, Rajou grabbed a handful of snow, made a snowball, and threw it at Harley, who quickly made a snowball of her own. Rajou tried to duck, lost his balance, and fell flat on his face. Together, they burst into laughter.

Stopping in the middle of the trail, Shelby turned to them and shouted, "This isn't a time to play games. Soon it will be night and we won't be able to continue."

Harley and Rajou picked up their pace. The sky was already dark when the wind started to howl. They walked for a long while, the heavy, blinding snow up to their knees and not another soul in sight. Harley felt like they were in another world, an utterly uncaring and menacing place that could swallow them whole, leaving no trace behind.

"We'll stop here for the night," Shelby shouted against the wind, pointing at a large boulder that had formed a natural roof. Rajou shook his head. "We can keep walking. There's still some light and we can make it to Bhojbasa."

Harley tried to assess the conditions. She couldn't see a foot in front of her. Turning to Rajou, she said, "I agree with Shelby. We must stay here for the night. It's too dangerous to keep going."

Shelby began pulling tent pegs out of his backpack, and Rajou sprang into action, helping him clear the snow that had piled up around the boulder. As she joined them, Harley realized they were in deep trouble, stuck in the Himalayas in the middle of a blizzard, without any chance of rescue. She recalled Shelby's warning back in New York, about the dangers involved in such a journey to the mountains, and tried to focus on what the swami had said about Shelby's life and hers being linked through her father, who was still looking out for her. *I'm here because I need to be here. Everything happens for a reason*, she told herself as she helped to clear the snow.

Night was falling fast, dark and frozen, without a moon or stars. Arranging their sleeping bags side by side, Shelby ordered them to stay with their coats on but their shoes off. He stuffed the shoes into a large plastic bag, and the three of them crawled into their sleeping bags, the wind howling in their ears. Harley's feet and fingers were frozen. Shelby asked her to remove her socks, then stretched out her feet and placed them under Rajou's shirt, against the skin of his stomach. After a few minutes Harley felt herself beginning to thaw.

The three of them lay huddled in their coats together, sharing breaths inside the improvised shelter they had made for themselves. Shelby passed around a small bottle of whiskey, and after a few sips Harley felt a lot better. She was cold but not frozen. She realized that Shelby and Rajou needed to be with her in this place, on this adventure. What would have happened if she had embarked on this journey alone? Would she have survived this blizzard? Would she have disappeared forever like her father? Surrounded by their body heat, Harley felt safe and protected, even in the eye of the storm. In no time, all three of them fell asleep, exhausted by the physical and mental effort they had expended during the day.

Morning broke in pale light. Harley was the first to wake up. So as not to disturb Shelby and Rajou's sleep, she lay without moving. *We're lucky to be alive,* she thought, grateful that they had not frozen to death. Harley remembered her promise to Uncle Charlie, not to take unnecessary risks and to turn back if she came across any danger. She now realized one cannot always turn back; there are real risks in life when one takes on something extraordinary. Peeking outside, Harley saw that the blizzard had wound down. Heavy snow covered the valley, but mountaintops could be seen from behind the thick veil of fog. Soon Rajou and Shelby were awake as well.

"Should we keep going or return to Gangotri?" Rajou asked.

Harley and Shelby exchanged a quick glance.

"We'll keep going," Shelby said.

After some water and biscuits, they gathered up their belongings and began treading through the thick snow.

The trail was still hard to make out, but they stuck to the mountain's slope and moved forward at a steady pace. With not a single soul to be seen, they felt as if they were utterly on their own, at the end of the world. After walking a bit further, they came across a row of huts.

"Bhojbasa, over there!" Rajou pointed.

This was their last stop before the climb to the glacier and Harley let out a sigh of relief. When they arrived at the modest guesthouse, the manager was utterly surprised to see them. Rajou told him how they had gotten trapped in the blizzard and the manager clicked his tongue and shook his head from side to side in disbelief.

"He says we were very lucky," Rajou translated as the manager spoke. "If the temperatures had fallen by just a few more degrees, we would have frozen to death."

The manager led them to a large room and brought a bucket of hot water. They removed their socks and hung them and their wet sleeping bags over the fireplace. As they placed their hands and feet inside the large bucket, they were overcome with exhaustion. Over hot tea they decided to use what remained of the day for rest. They would leave for the glacier and ice cave in the morning, accompanied by a local guide.

"I don't know what we would have done without you," Harley said to Shelby, regaining some of her strength. "We would have died in that blizzard."

Rajou nodded in agreement.

"I was in a similar situation before, that's all. It was simply my turn to guide *you*," Shelby replied.

Harley recalled the Principle of Eighteen. "Could you tell us more about the Mentor stage?" she asked.

Shelby looked encouraged by the request. "The Mentor stage begins around the time we turn fifty," he explained. "After having invested time and effort building and creating, mentors look for a way to deliver the knowledge and experience they have accumulated to young people who are just starting out."

"Could you give me an example?"

"Consider a successful novelist. She continues to write but instead of focusing only on herself, she pens a book on how one can become a better novelist, or leads a book club in her neighborhood, or teaches creative writing at a local college. She begins sharing her knowledge with people who are at the exploring stage."

"And what if she just continues to write novels without mentoring others?" Harley asked.

"In that case, she's betraying the thing that made her successful in the first place. We are all dependent on other people to show us the way."

Shelby lit his pipe. The sweet smoke wending through the room reminded Harley of Uncle Charlie. Shelby's eyes were nearly shut, and it seemed he was about to fall asleep. A moment later he turned to look out the frozen window, his gaze traveling back in time.

"It all began here in Bhojbasa," he said quietly.

CHAPTER 15

HARLEY TENSED UP IN HER seat. Rajou stared at Shelby. Without looking at them, Shelby began to recount what happened on that fateful night, the last time he saw Jack, Harley's father, alive. He pointed toward the window and spoke.

"It was a similar blizzard. The only difference was that it had been raging for a few days already, not letting up for a moment, piling massive amounts of snow across the valley." He looked around the small room, barely noticing Harley and Rajou. "As soon as the storm started, the other travelers packed their bags and headed back to Gangotri. Jack and I were the only Western tourists left, like two stubborn guards unwilling to abandon their post. I figured that we were going to wait until the storm passed, and then head back to Gangotri, but Jack had other plans . . ." Shelby stopped talking and puffed on his pipe.

"I told Jack it was time to give up and head back to safety, but he insisted on reaching the glacier no matter what. I held my ground, telling him that such a decision would be utterly reckless. I even brought up Sarah and . . ." He glanced at Harley, as if surprised to see her with him, in the same desolate room, during another blizzard in the Himalayas.

"And then what happened?" asked Harley impatiently. She didn't like the direction of what was unfolding in front of her.

"We had a real fight, for the first time in our many years of friendship," answered Shelby. "Jack argued that we hadn't made it all the way here only to go back empty-handed. We both knew we couldn't stay in Bhojbasa since the heavy snow would make it impossible to return to Gangotri. The window of opportunity was closing fast. A quick decision needed to be made. Jack's plan for us was to climb the glacier at the first crack of dawn, reach the ice cave, and then head back to Gangotri."

Shelby stopped speaking and looked out the frozen window. After a few moments he continued.

"Jack paced this room like a caged tiger. He wasn't willing to give up. Every ordinary person would have understood the risk involved, but Jack was no ordinary person. He pushed himself to do things few people dare do in life. With every success, his confidence grew. I told him he was playing with fire, that he was like Icarus—flying too close to the sun. He said that most people think Icarus paid for his sins of pride and vanity, but that he saw him as a trailblazer, someone who wasn't willing to accept the usual limitations people placed on themselves. At that point I lashed out and asked Jack if he was prepared to die. I'll never forget what happened next."

Smoke rings rose toward the ceiling, irritating Harley's eyes, but she didn't bother to wipe them. Removing the pipe from his mouth, Shelby stuffed more tobacco leaves inside with the stem and said, "Jack halted his frantic pacing across the room, walked right up to me, and said that he had to do it. And then he quoted a line from Rilke."

Preemptively, Harley recited the words: "Our deepest fears are like dragons guarding our deepest treasure." Rajou gave her a puzzled look, but Shelby nodded.

"For him, reaching the ice cave took on a spiritual meaning. He felt that this cave, the source of the blessed Ganges River, would unlock something deep within him. I remember him saying that "getting to the source of this river is like getting to the source of my soul.""

Shelby choked back his words. "Your father took my hand and asked me to look out for Sarah and you if anything happened to him. I dismissed his request, telling him that nothing would happen since we were both going back to Gangotri in the morning. I genuinely believed it. But when I woke up early in the morning, he was gone."

Shelby's words hung heavily in the smoky air. Shelby continued talking, as if relieved to tell the entire story after all these years. "The blizzard lasted for one more day, too long for the rescue team I had organized to turn up anything. In their official report they wrote that Jack had likely fallen into one of those horribly deep crevices in the glacier." In a cracked voice, Shelby concluded, "I should've stayed up all night. I could have prevented it."

Rajou turned to him. "Do you remember what the swami told you? Do the best you can but don't take responsibility for other people's destinies." Harley approached Shelby and hugged him, but Shelby remained frozen in place, stiff and unresponsive.

"I can't lie to you anymore," he finally said, as if a spell had been broken. "There was something else that happened that night, something that I have kept in the dark all these years."

"I'm listening," said Harley cautiously.

"The truth is that I had agreed to climb the glacier with Jack. He convinced me, and I didn't want him to go out there on his own." Shelby stopped for a quick furtive look at Harley's face, but she showed no emotion.

He coughed and then continued, "I had brought a bottle of whiskey with me to celebrate reaching the ice cave. But now that our plans had changed, and we were going to head back toward Gangotri right after the glacier, I suggested breaking out the bottle. Jack wasn't much of a drinker, so I ended up consuming more than my fair share. Jack kept telling me to take it easy, but I was under so much stress. . ." He didn't continue, staring into the worn carpet below him without saying anything.

"And you didn't wake up in time to join Jack for the morning hike," Rajou filled in the blanks.

Shelby nodded heavily and after a few minutes continued, his speech becoming slower. "After I finished off the bottle, I don't remember anything else from that night. I woke up at noon. Jack probably tried to wake me, but then gave up and left on his own. I failed him, and failed you, Harley." With tears streaming down his cheeks, he looked up at her, his eyes filled with unfathomable shame.

Harley's eyes remained dry. There was nothing to be said right now. She could understand the source of Shelby's shame and why he had hidden it all these years, but for some strange reason she didn't blame him for passing out that evening. What struck her instead was the reckless way her father had conducted himself. She understood from Shelby's descriptions of him during this journey that her father liked to rebel against the norm and resisted following in other people's footsteps. But Shelby's recent story pointed to a different side of her father's personality—an irresponsible, impulsive one. With one reckless decision, someone could jeopardize what they had worked for their entire lives, leaving their loved ones with a never-ending sense of loss. This was a difficult thought for Harley to digest.

Shelby turned to Harley. "You know your mother severed all ties with me," he said, smiling bitterly. "God knows I tried getting back in touch with her, but she was unwilling to leave even a small crack through which we could reestablish our friendship. I spent years feeling guilty for not fulfilling your father's final wish, which was to look after you and Sarah. When I saw you in class for the first time, I couldn't believe it. You were so grown up. Of course, I couldn't tell you what had happened, even though there were times I almost did." Harley squeezed Shelby's hand and he looked at her with gratitude.

After a light dinner they all spread their sleeping bags onto the dusty thin mattresses in the room and said good night. The following morning, weather permitting, they would climb the glacier with the help of a local guide and reach the ice cave. Harley tossed and turned, unable to calm herself and fall asleep. She wondered how well we truly know those around us. She wondered about the secrets they kept hidden deep inside, sometimes forever. She thought of how she had hidden her own secrets from her travel companions, her mother, and Uncle Charlie. It occurred to her that Rajou was the only one not trying to hide anything; and it was this thought that finally caused her eyelids to flutter shut.

She dreamed again of climbing the glacier.

The wind howled in her ears and the moon was full. She struggled to reach the flat plane leading to the ice cave, straining her muscles to the breaking point. Finally, giving it her all, she made it onto the plane of ice. She looked around, the mountains towering above her. At a distance she saw the wall of ice with the dark opening leading to the source of the Ganges. Near the ice cave she saw a sitting figure wrapped in a white cape. She approached it gingerly, ignoring the warning signs circling like invisible eagles in the thin air. She tried to remind herself she was dreaming but everything around her looked and felt real.

Hesitantly, she called out her father's name, but the figure did not respond. With more determination, she tapped its shoulder, prompting the figure to swiftly rise from his place and turn to her. To her amazement, Harley saw that the strange being was herself. The combination of the white cape and ice all around was uncanny, as if this being might disappear into its surroundings at any moment.

The mysterious figure examined her for a long moment, her face shining in ethereal whiteness, and gently said, "Did you bring it?"

"Bring what?" she asked in confusion.

"The gift from Father."

Harley understood. She removed the golden key from around her neck and handed it to her other self, who looked at the key, and then at Harley, in silence. The moon softly lit her face. Time now took on a deep and slow dimension, like an old plank of wood from a ship gradually sinking into the depths of the ocean. The world existed only for them. As if hypnotized, Harley stared at her figure holding the key. Finally, the figure spoke again.

"Have you learned how to use it?" she asked, looking through her.

"I don't understand . . ." Harley answered.

"Have you used the key to open your heart?"

Harley took a small step back. "I'm trying to," she said hesitantly. "It's a lot harder than I thought."

"It's a lot harder than you thought," the otherworldly figure slowly repeated her words, as if trying to make sense of them. She weighed the key in her hand a few times, and Harley noticed that her fingers were almost translucent. It seemed that her other self was debating whether to keep the key or return it to Harley. Eventually she handed it back and said, "I will be waiting for you."

Without a goodbye, the figure turned her head and sat down in front of the cave with her legs crossed. Harley asked, with a sense of urgency, how she would be able to find her again, but the figure did not respond. A powerful wind kicked up and it began to snow. The wind whistled in Harley's ears, sounding alarm bells, but she ignored them and stood still. She knew it was dangerous to remain on the glacier, and that this was what her father must have felt during the last moments of his life. She told herself she had to wake her other self now and get clear answers to all the questions that were nagging at her.

The wind began to resist her as she struggled to remain in place. Her breathing grew heavy, but she refused to climb off the glacier. Explosions sounded and cracks appeared in the ice wall above the cave. Her other self suddenly stood up, the white cape twirling around her. It pointed to the plane of ice behind them. Harley heard a single word in her head: *Go.*

She turned back and began running. The fissure in the wall was so wide now that it threatened to split it in half. To the sound of ice cracking, Harley saw the figure disappear. She continued to run. A huge block of ice dropped with a deafening thud, splintering across the ice plane, sending large shards everywhere. Looking back, Harley saw that the entire glacier was beginning to crumble. A voice inside her said, *You should not have come here but you insisted. Now you must pay the price.*

As she ran, Harley remembered the sunny winter day she'd spent sledding with her father. She recalled the terror that had grabbed hold of her when she first looked down the steep slope, and then the safety she felt rushing down on the sled, her father holding her in his protective embrace. Her heart was beating at record speed. At the edge of the ice plane, she paused. A dark abyss opened before her. She bid farewell to every person she had ever loved, then leapt into the gaping chasm. She thought of how she had done everything in her power to find her father and how, during her search, she had connected to a mysterious spot in her heart that was strong and full of life. *If I must die now, at least I know I did not let myself down*, she thought.

She plummeted through the air, then slammed into a snowy slope and began to quickly roll down it. Hurtling forward, she felt her ears ringing and the taste of blood in her mouth. As she lifted her head, Harley heard her father's voice saying encouragingly, "That wasn't so scary now, was it?" Buried beneath the avalanche, she began to laugh hysterically, incredulous that she had made it to the end of the slope and that she was still alive.

She struggled to find a way to the surface and eventually managed to extricate herself. She shook the snow from her clothes, surprised that she didn't feel any pain, and as she began to walk, she saw that this time she was leaving tracks in the snow. Next to her tracks were a second set, wider and more visible. Harley tried to make out who was walking in her midst and suddenly felt a hand touch her shoulder. She screamed and opened her eyes. Rajou was standing above her, shaking her awake.

"Are you alright?" he asked, looking concerned.

"What happened?"

"You were talking in your sleep. When I came near you, you woke up screaming. I couldn't tell if I heard *leap!* or *leave!*"

"I'm fine, Rajou. I just had another strange dream." She shook her head as if to expel the memory of it.

"Do you want to talk about it?"

"I'm fine," Harley said again, and offered Rajou a tired smile. "Good night."

CHAPTER 16

THEY WOKE UP EARLY. HARLEY felt tired from the night before, but after two cups of hot tea and some oatmeal she regained her energy. They packed what they needed to climb the glacier and gathered outside near the local guide, a quiet man with a furry mustache who wore a tattered grey coat with a faded fur collar. The guide began leading them toward the glacier without any explanations about the path ahead. He knew the way and led them with confidence.

Despite the thin air and high altitude, Harley's mind seemed clearer than ever. The guide pointed out a few avalanches triggered by the blizzard, the blocks of ice resembling scattered chess pieces played by giants. With labored breath, they advanced in measured steps. From time to time, creaking sounds from the glacier could be heard. There was a joy in each of Harley's steps, even though her nose was so cold she could no longer feel it.

And then, eventually, they made it to the ice cave. Towering mountains surrounded them in a regal, chilling silence. The holy cave was deep inside the belly of the glacier, with clear water flowing through it into a small pool made of rocks. Recalling the mighty Ganges, Harley couldn't believe it all began right here, in a mysterious pool of water. They turned to embrace each other, thrilled and relieved to have arrived at their destination.

Each one of them became immersed in their own thoughts. After a few minutes, Shelby smiled. His eyes beaming with excitement, he addressed Harley: "I feel your father's presence with us now. He is happy that we made it this far and is bidding us farewell," he said.

Harley closed her eyes, trying to summon the same feeling.

Shelby continued, "The fact that you are here with me now, in this special place, means so much. I can't tell you how many nights I dreamed that one day, somehow, something like this might transpire."

As she stood in front of the frozen river at the heart of the glacier, Harley thought of the dreams she'd had about this place. The cave looked as she had imagined it but there was no figure wrapped in a cape at the entrance. She tried to conjure her father's face but the image that entered her mind was blurry. Touching the golden key around her neck, she recalled the strange man on the night bus from Delhi to Rishikesh, and his odd instructions about finding a golden key at the bottom of a lake that would lead her to a life of happiness.

Turning to Shelby and Rajou, she repeated the man's cryptic words about needing to wait for the winds to stop blowing before she could dive in and find the key. They both smiled at the same moment.

"You tell her, Rajou," Shelby said and patted Rajou affectionately on the back.

"It's an ancient Buddhist fable," Rajou said. "The lake represents your thoughts, the way they come and go without you having any control over them."

"And the key?" Harley asked.

"The key represents true understanding."

"Of what?"

"First of yourself, of your true nature," Rajou explained. "Then, an understanding of the world around you. If you're unable to calm your mind and truly relax, the waves created by the winds will continue to conceal the golden key. Only when your mind is calm will the key reveal itself."

"In all its glory," Shelby added. "Bright and shining, waiting for you to use it."

Harley considered this new perspective. "Meaning there is no real lake, no real golden key?" she offered her interpretation.

"That's right. The lake represents your mind, the thoughts and emotions that control all of us, and the key represents what's hidden in your heart," Shelby said. "Don't forget it is not enough to merely find the key that will open your heart. What matters is what you do after you unlock it—living according to what your heart tells you, even when you're not sure it's the right thing to do."

Harley chuckled. "I can't believe I thought the man meant a real key and real treasure," she said.

"Don't worry, you're not the only one. The expression *fool's gold* exists for a reason," Shelby said, chuckling in return.

Harley removed the golden key from around her neck and examined the Sanskrit on the back. She thought about the meaning of the inscription and the perilous journey to this mysterious place and felt inspired to break through whatever roadblocks lay in her path. Opening her heart to the virginal view around her, Harley was flooded with immense gratitude. She was finally at peace with herself and with the mighty glacier that had taken her father's life so many years ago. Clasping the key in the palm of her hand, she said, "This is for you, Dad. You never believed in boundaries. You always tried to break through the walls around you. You are the one who is truly boundless."

She kissed the key and cast it toward the bubbling current. Silently, the three of them followed the small key as it arched through the air, glistening in the sun, before sinking into the small pool, the source of the great Ganges.

Evening was approaching. Soon they arrived at a tall flat surface broken by meandering pools of water: Tapovan, according to Shelby. Lifting his arms, he pointed to the beautiful jagged Shivling Mountain, which overlooked a small meadow. He pulled out the tent from his backpack and the guide began pitching his as well.

Harley approached Shelby. "Would you mind sleeping in the guide's tent tonight?" she asked gently. He gave her a look of surprise, which quickly softened into a smile. "Of course," he said. As night fell, Harley cuddled with Rajou inside his sleeping bag. His long arms enveloped her, and his soft lips kissed her forehead, her lips, her neck. She turned inside the narrow space, hopelessly trying to wrap her arms around him, and they both burst out laughing.

"It feels like the two of us were meant to meet; that fate brought us together," she whispered.

"The first time I saw you I knew I wanted to be with you," Rajou whispered back.

Harley smiled in the dark. A cold wind blew around them. Burying her head in Rajou's collarbone, she quickly fell into a warm sleep.

CHAPTER 17

IN THE MORNING, AFTER HOT tea and biscuits, they folded their tents and began the journey back to Gangotri. Two days later they found themselves in Rajou's ashram in Haridwar. After a quick dinner Shelby retired to his room and Harley and Rajou stood outside on the large balcony, watching the meandering river in the distance. Harley felt restless and tense, knowing she would soon have to part ways with Rajou. He held her hand tightly, as if he were thinking the same.

"You know . . ."

"Yes," he said.

Harley pursed her lips. "It won't be easy, picking up where I left off," she said, a quiet sadness washing over her.

"When will we see each other again?" he asked.

"I don't know." She answered, shaking her head from side to side.

Harley's heart sank when she thought of the immense distance that would soon come between them. That night they did not leave each other's side, trying to absorb enough warmth to nourish them for as long as possible.

In the morning, they woke up to the sound of a rooster crowing. A pale light had broken through the grey sky. Harley asked Rajou to meet her at the bus stop, grabbed her backpack, and walked toward the large lawn. Here she saw Shelby, sitting on the large white boulder and writing in his journal. When he saw her, he stopped writing and closed the journal.

"Good morning," he greeted Harley.

"Good morning," Harley replied without much enthusiasm.

"How'd you sleep?"

"Fine."

Two birds flew by, chasing each other silently and gracefully. Shelby stared at them for a minute and then asked, "And Rajou?"

"He'll come to the bus stop," Harley said. They began walking down the winding path toward the bridge, each of them immersed in their own thoughts. At one of the bends in the road, they took a sharp turn.

"Hellllooo snake!" the old woman screamed, shoving the snake into Shelby's surprised face. He jumped back and fell onto a pile of burlap sacks. Harley burst out laughing. She helped him up and paid the woman to have a photo taken with the snake. The woman thanked her with a toothless smile, uttered a quick sentence in Hindi, and returned to her usual ambush spot.

Before arriving at the bus stop, they came across a rangy barber standing next to a makeshift chair, a pair of long scissors in his hand. When he saw Shelby and his wild hair, he cocked his head and covered his mouth to conceal his smile. They stopped in front of the smiling barber as he began opening and closing his scissors, coaxing Shelby into the chair. After washing Shelby's hair with a bottle of hot water and a green, fragrant shampoo, the barber began to snip quickly and skillfully. Long locks fell around Shelby, a sight he happily beheld. The haircut made him look several years younger. Afterward, the barber shaved his face with careful movements, then massaged his head and snapped a towel around his neck. Finally, he rubbed Shelby's skin with a sweet-smelling ointment. Shelby stood up, ruddy-cheeked and energetic. He spread open his arms and called out, "I feel great!"

Harley smiled and thought, *This is what a man looks like after ridding himself of a heavy burden.* They continued their way until they found the bus to New Delhi. Shelby boarded it while Harley waited for Rajou near the large bridge. Starting to worry, she looked back at the ashram and saw Rajou running toward her. A minute later he reached her, panting heavily.

"Did you run all the way here?" Harley asked.

Rajou nodded. "Did the woman with the snake talk to you?" he asked her.

"She stopped me and told me you paid her handsomely. And she asked me to translate the sentence she shared with you."

Harley looked at him and asked with her eyes for him to go on.

"She wished for you to shed your worries, the same way her King Cobra sheds his skin, only to emerge stronger."

Harley smiled. Rajou's smile back made her heart sink. "I wish I could stay here with you," she said.

"Maybe for a nice sum the old woman can sell me a potion that will make it impossible for you to ever leave this place," he said, batting his long lashes.

They hugged and Harley felt his heart beating faster. "I have to go home," she said.

"I know." Rajou tightened his grip around her shoulders. "I'll never forget what we went through together. You'll always have a special place in my heart," he said.

A loud honk from the direction of the bus drowned out Harley's reply. She tried to speak again but the noise was deafening. Turning to see what the commotion was all about, she saw Shelby getting off the bus. He hurried toward them in a few quick steps, gave Rajou a tight hug, and said, "I know we'll see each other again. Take care of yourself."

Looking at Rajou all the while, Harley boarded the bus with Shelby. The bus began to pull away, honking loudly, creating a cloud of dust that filled the small platform. Through the dust Harley could see Rajou's slender figure waving goodbye. She tried waving back, but his dust-covered figure slowly disappeared, and Harley felt she was leaving a part of herself behind with Rajou and the Ganges River at the foot of the Himalayas.

The rest of the ride was uneventful. Shelby and Harley were incredibly tired and slept the whole way. When they arrived at Divya's house, Harley felt she had come full circle. Divya was no doubt surprised to see Shelby with Harley but did not say anything. Harley introduced Shelby as her university professor who was in India on an academic tour. Divya's family warmly welcomed him, and as soon as the two girls had a spare moment Divya led Harley to an isolated corner in the expansive garden. Under the shade of a huge Ficus tree, they sat on a bench. A light breeze blew, and a single bird chirped monotonously from above. A monkey swung on a branch nearby, and Harley could swear it was the same one that had scattered all her possessions.

Divya turned to Harley, her eyes beaming with excitement. "Can you explain to me what Professor Shelby is doing here? And did you find out what happened to your father?"

Harley told Divya about Rajou, their sudden meeting with Shelby, and their whole ordeal on the way to the glacier.

"That's an incredible story!" Divya exclaimed and took Harley's hand. "How do you feel about what you learned?"

"I'm still processing everything," Harley replied. "I've experienced so many things. What I know for certain is that I'm glad I went on this journey."

"And what about Rajou?"

Harley blushed. "What do you mean?"

"It sounds like the two of you have a special bond."

"That's true. I just don't know what's going to happen with us. When I said goodbye, I felt like I was making a huge mistake, that I should stay with him."

"That's called love," Divya laughed. "What are you going to do?"

"Right now, I'm going back to New York. I have no idea what's going to happen after that."

"Well, you should start by calling your mother," Divya said with a smile.

Back inside the house, Harley heard the relief in her mother's voice over the phone. They talked for a few minutes, but Harley sensed that part of the intimate bond they used to share was lost. She realized that holding onto lies for too long begins to poison your relationships with those closest to you. She was eager to share all her adventures with her mother, but she knew it was something she had to do in person. She told her mother everything was fine and that she couldn't wait to tell her about all her experiences during the trip. She did not elaborate about the journey to Gangotri or meeting Professor Shelby.

In the living room, Shelby and Divya's father were in the middle of a lively conversation about Indian mythology, and Divya was having a pillow fight with her two little brothers. Harley felt ready to return home and start a new chapter in her life. She got on the phone again and called Uncle Charlie.

"I'm coming home tomorrow," she said. "Flight 1818 out of New Delhi."

"Are you alright?" Uncle Charlie asked.

"Everything's fine," Harley replied, then added, "And Charlie?"

"Yes?"

"I found the hiker who was with Dad when he disappeared. The report you got about that other person was true."

There was a long silence on the other end of the line. She heard Charlie breathing fast. After he collected himself, he said, "I'll pick you up from the airport."

CHAPTER 18

IN THE EVENING DIVYA'S FAMILY driver drove Harley and Shelby to the airport. The flight was half empty and they fell asleep as soon as the plane took off, waking up as the flight attendant was serving breakfast. Sipping her hot coffee, Harley felt excited and nervous about coming back home and the important conversations she needed to have with her mother and Uncle Charlie.

After they landed, they went to pick up their luggage together. "Charlie is picking me up," Harley hesitantly informed Shelby.

"Charlie . . ." Shelby repeated somberly. "All these years he was looking for a lead about what happened in the Himalayas . . . all these years I could have spared him the trouble . . ."

"Remember, we're turning over a new leaf, Mark," Harley reminded him.

"I guess you're going to tell him what happened."

"Yes. He needs to know. So does my mother."

Shelby nodded. "You know, I never told your mother that I was totally drunk that evening, and that I woke up too late . . ." his words trailed off. Harley felt a strange need to comfort Shelby, even as she wondered whether her dad might be alive today had Shelby stayed sober that night.

"I'll tell them how brave you were on this adventure with Rajou and me," she said, and squeezed Shelby's hand.

"Tell Charlie I'm sorry," he called out as she walked toward the exit.

Harley turned back. "I understand that it might be hard for you to talk to my mother, but you should talk to Charlie and tell him what happened," she said.

Shelby looked at Harley skeptically and said, "If I remember Charlie, he wouldn't be very excited to talk to me." *Mark's probably right to dread this meeting*, thought Harley to herself. She hugged Shelby without saying anything. Outside the terminal, a driver in a black suit and green tie was holding a sign with her name on it. Taking Harley's luggage, he led the way to the parking lot. They arrived at a fancy black car; the driver opened the back door, and Harley got in next to Charlie. When he hugged her, she saw dark circles under his eyes. Harley stretched out on the comfy leather seat, thinking how nice it felt to be so close to the ground.

Examining his niece, Charlie said, "Thank God, you look well."

"And you look tired," she said.

"I am. I couldn't stop thinking about you. Did you keep your promise not to take any unnecessary risks?"

Harley considered all that she had gone through and said, "I tried. But there were a few times I didn't use good judgment."

Charley sighed. "Well, at least you're here now, safe and sound. I have to admit you surprised me when you called from New Delhi and told me you found out what had happened to Jack."

Harley observed how old he looked, almost as old as Shelby before he left for India.

"Dad was not traveling alone," she said quietly.

Charlie stuffed his pipe and lit it. Pale blue smoke curled inside the car and Harley opened the window.

"The pilgrim's story really was true," he said.

"Yes." Debating the best way to tell him what she knew, Harley settled on: "Charlie, the person who was with my father on that trip was Dr. Mark Shelby."

"Mark Shelby?" he gasped. "Your father's closest friend?"

Harley told him about having met Shelby unexpectedly in Gangotri; their travels together to the glacier; his resourcefulness during the blizzard; and what she had learned about Jack. She didn't disclose that Shelby had been drunk that fateful evening. When she finished, Charlie was quiet for a long time. He looked out toward the river flowing by the side of the road. Then he said, "My worst fear was that he was murdered or duped in some way. How do you feel about what you learned?"

"I've had a lot of time to think about it. At first, I was angry at Dad for his recklessness, at Mom for not telling me the whole truth, and at Shelby for his elaborate lies. I felt like I had been deceived all these years." She took a deep breath. "Now I understand we don't really have control over what other people do, even the people we're closest to."

"You didn't have to travel all the way to the Himalayas to find that out," Charlie said, and snickered. "I could have told you that when we met at my house."

"Maybe you're right," Harley said. "What matters is that I learned how much our actions can affect other people, for better or for worse."

"You're talking about Shelby," Charley said, his expression severe.

She had actually meant her father. "Mark asked me to tell you he was sorry," she told her uncle, relaying Shelby's apology.

Shelby shook his head. "It's too late to apologize. Too many years, too many sleepless nights."

"You don't want to talk to him?"

"He should do his soul searching on his own. I'm not about to reconnect with the one person who was there, but not brave enough to tell me about it. That kind of thing is unforgivable."

"Unforgivable?"

"That's right. And I don't wish to discuss this matter further." His reaction jolted Harley. After regaining her composure, she said, "I think he's already paid enough for his secret."

"I don't care!" Charlie exploded. "He knew what happened to my only brother and chose to hide it. Don't you understand how serious that is?"

She did, very well, but was surprised by the intensity of Charlie's feelings, and hoped her mother would have a better reaction. The big car with its quiet engine kept moving forward. As they passed a large bridge, Harley considered its reflection in the river.

Charlie took a few deep breaths. "I'm sorry Harley. This has nothing to do with you. It's just that I've been searching all these years, and all along the answer was so close by."

Harley placed her hand on his and soon her uncle became calm again. She started telling him about the Principle of Eighteen, and that her parents and Shelby had worked on it together. In so doing, they had created an original framework for living a full life, comprised of five interconnected stages. Charlie listened intently, his head bent slightly toward his niece.

"So according to this theory I should be a mentor to younger people?" he asked.

"That's right!" said Harley enthusiastically. "You could share your life lessons, everything that you've learned along the way, with people who are just starting out."

Charlie puffed on his cigar and said, "And what did your dad get out of all that work?" Harley did not respond. For some reason, her thoughts went back to Rajou, the way his smile was always at the ready even in the most unexpected places. She missed him terribly. Without thinking too much, she turned to look at her uncle and said, "There's something else. I didn't plan for it, but I fell in love during this trip."

Charlie pulled his hand away from her as if bitten by a snake.

"That bastard Shelby!" he cried in disbelief.

"*What?! No!*" said Harley in confusion, shaking her head vigorously from side to side.

Charlie laughed, but there was no warmth in his smile. He was breathing hard now, his head turned down, and Harley could hear him say, "He's going to pay dearly for this!"

"Charlie, it wasn't Shelby!" cried Harley. "I fell in love with a young Indian man who came with me to the glacier!"

Charlie looked at her with squinted eyes, as if trying to determine the truth of her words. His eyes met her steady stare and he realized that his hatred of Shelby had led him on this wild- goose chase. He exhaled the air from his lungs and was quiet for a few minutes before looking at Harley.

"I'm sorry, kid. This has been a bit much for me. Can you tell me more about this young man?"

Harley told Charlie about the gentle way Rajou treated her during the short time they'd spent together. Charlie nodded in approval.

"This Rajou seems like a fine young man to me," he said and chuckled. Harley squeezed his hand in gratitude. Gently pulling his hand away from hers, Charlie removed a long envelope from his jacket pocket. "This is for you," he said. Harley accepted the envelope. It was so slight; it didn't feel like there was anything in it. Opening it, she took out a thin piece of paper. In the dim light of the car, it was impossible to decipher what was written on it. "What does it say?" she asked. Charlie flipped on a dome light. Moving the paper into the light, Harley gasped when she saw what it was: a check for a million dollars made out in her name. Her mind drew a blank as she sat there staring at it. She couldn't possibly accept such an enormous gift.

Charlie observed her with a slight smile, then took her hand again and said, "Put all of those thoughts you're having aside. You're the one who solved this mystery. You're entitled to the reward money."

She began to protest—the thought of keeping the check was absurd—but then remembered what Charlie had told her in his mansion about people not knowing how to receive the precious gifts that life sometimes gives them. Hugging him, she said simply, still in a daze, "Thank you, Charlie."

"I'm the one who should be thanking you," he said.

Harley looked at the check again. She had no idea what to do with that much money and knew her mother would insist that she immediately return it. Putting it back in the envelope, she carefully resealed it. Then she handed it back to a confused Charlie.

"I'm giving you the money for safekeeping until I know what to do with it."

He smiled in admiration. "I see you learned quite few things on this adventure of yours," he said.

As her home appeared within view, Harley felt the anticipation of seeing her mother again wash over her like a warm wave. Charlie leaned toward her, clasped both her cheeks, and said, "I'm proud of you."

She smiled, kissed her uncle goodbye, and got out of the car, whose door was held open by the driver. Joe, the doorman, regarded his tenant in amazement as he opened the door to the building.

"I see you're moving up in life, Ms. Green," he said. "Welcome home."

Harley smiled. "Good to see you again, Joe," she replied.

She rang the doorbell. Her mother answered and they hugged each other tightly for a long moment. After eating a delicious chocolate cake, they sat on the sofa overlooking the Hudson. Harley had anticipated this moment for a long time, rehearsing in her mind how she would tell her mother she had gone in search of her father and did not stay in New Delhi with Divya. Now, however, when she looked into Sarah's eyes, she couldn't get the words out. Her mom hugged her again, and Harley could sense her relief in having her daughter back home in one piece. "My daughter," Sarah said and kissed Harley on her forehead. She touched Harley's hair and smiled.

"You can't imagine how much I missed you," her mother said.

"Me too," was all Harley could manage. Sarah looked puzzled, sensing something was wrong. Harley thought of what Mark Shelby had told her, about the limited time one must reveal something kept hidden, and how after that time is up the lie becomes hard and impenetrable, like a fossil. Shaking her head, she said, "I didn't tell you the whole truth about my trip to India."

Sarah stared at her.

Harley continued. "I didn't just stay in New Delhi. I went to the Himalayan Mountains, to the place where Dad disappeared."

For some reason Sarah did not appear particularly surprised. Perhaps she had known about Harley's plan all along? The thought quickly flashed through Harley's mind. When her mother still did not say anything, Harley went on, "I didn't want to tell you because I knew you would try to stop me, but it was something I had to do."

Harley told her mother the whole story, from the moment she'd arrived at Divya's home in New Delhi.

Her mother smiled at the part about meeting Rajou and the special connection they developed. When she got to the part about meeting Shelby in Gangotri, she saw her mother turn pale.

"Mark Shelby," she mumbled under her breath. She cleared her throat and headed toward the kitchen. Harley followed her.

"He saved Rajou and me during a blizzard." Harley went on to describe the adventure. Her mother hugged her tightly again. "And then, when we made it to Bhojbasa, Mark told Rajou and me what really happened to Dad."

Her mother became even paler. "What do you mean?" she asked in a whisper.

"When they made it to the glacier, a serious blizzard was raging," Harley said. "All the supplies they had brought with them were running out and they needed to backtrack to avoid getting stuck in the snow. The night before Dad disappeared, they argued about whether they should go back or not. They didn't come to an agreement and went to bed. Dad woke up incredibly early in the morning and left for the glacier, solo, without a companion or guide, and without informing Mark," Harley said.

"And Mark was simply asleep that whole time?"

Harley cleared her throat. "He couldn't have imagined Dad would walk out on his own in the middle of the freezing night."

"I already know all of this," Harley's mother said quietly. "That's what Mark told me when he returned from

India. I always felt it didn't really matter. At the end of the day, he made it home safely, while Jack . . ."

Sarah sat quietly, her eyes wandering from the picture of the huge wave in the middle of the ocean to her only daughter. Eventually she said, "I also didn't tell you everything I knew about Dad's disappearance. I think it's too late now to get angry with you for everything you kept from me. You made it home safe and that's what matters."

Harley nodded. Once her mother had decided to keep the truth from her daughter, it became almost impossible to tell Harley, all these years later, that her university professor had been involved in her father's final adventure. There was one other thing that bothered Harley. It was the same thing that Charlie had asked about on the way back from the airport. "Mom," she gently said, "I also called Charlie and told him all of this."

Sarah remained silent.

Harley continued, "You told Charlie about Gangotri, but for some reason you never mentioned anything about Mark. Charlie spent a fortune trying to figure out what happened to Dad, and you . . ."

Her mother interrupted her. "How well do you know Charlie?"

"He's my uncle," Harley quickly replied.

"That's true, but I don't think you understand his world and the rules he lives by."

"What do you mean?"

Sarah looked at her daughter and pursed her lips, as if to stop them from elaborating. "I was afraid that if Charlie knew Mark was with Jack and didn't do everything he could have to save him, he might hurt him in some way."

"Charlie would never do something like that," Harley said confidently.

Her mother snickered and lit a cigarette. Harley was surprised. She knew her mother had quit smoking years before. Gesticulating weakly with the hand holding her cigarette, she quietly said, "I was confused and vulnerable after your father disappeared. I didn't want to talk to anyone; didn't trust anyone. After Mark told me what had happened, I wanted nothing more to do with him."

"But it's been years since Dad's disappearance. You could have told Charlie; you could have given Mark another chance. Both loved Dad and have been suffering since he disappeared, each of them in his own way. Isn't it time to reach out to them?"

Sarah ignored the question, put out her cigarette, went to the kitchen table, and returned with a thin envelope. Harley looked at the envelope and saw the familiar King's Crown of Columbia University.

"What is it?" she asked.

"Open it."

She opened the envelope and took out a sheet of paper. The letter congratulated her on having been accepted to the prestigious graduate architecture school, along with a partial scholarship. Harley smiled and her mother smiled back at her.

"It all worked," said Sarah, hugging her daughter. "I am so proud of you, the hard work you put in all these years. This is your ticket to a bright future."

Harley considered her mother's words. One part of her wanted to agree with her mother and avoid the conflict, but another wiser part begged her to speak up.

"I'm grateful for this amazing opportunity. Truly am. But . . ."

"But what"?

Harley took several deep breathes.

"This is committing too much at this stage, before I even get a chance to see if being an architect is what I really want to do with the rest of my life."

Her mother stared at her.

Harley continued, "I want to know that I am doing the right thing with my career. I felt more alive during my adventure in India than at any other time in my life."

"I can understand that. A foreign country, the landscape, the people, the experiences you had, the strong emotions you felt. All that is behind you now. But this . . ." Sarah said in an urgent tone, pointing at the letter, "this is an opportunity you simply can't miss!"

Harley decided to be more direct. Leaning forward, she looked straight into her mother's eyes and said, "Mom, Shelby told me about the Principle of Eighteen that you two developed with Dad. The different life stages really made a lot of sense to me, and I plan on going out and exploring the world and my place in it for the next eighteen years, until I turn thirty-six."

Harley's mother was stunned into silence. Harley waited patiently.

"The Principle of Eighteen . . ." Sarah said, repeating her daughter's words. It seemed that these words carried her deep into the past, and Harley waited quietly for her mother to come back to her senses. A faint smile appeared on Sarah's face.

"The research we'd done was so promising. We believed that this principle could change the way people view their lives, bringing joy and optimism to countless individuals who would find purpose and structure under this original model of personal development."

"I know what you mean," said Harley. "Both Rajou and I were quite taken by the implications for our lives if we were to follow this principle."

Sarah frowned about the new direction their conversation had taken.

"You do realize we never completed our research? The partial results we gathered from the interviews we conducted were quite promising, but we never published a paper anywhere."

"That doesn't matter to me," Harley said. "What matters is that this helps me make sense of my life and form a long-term plan I can use. I now have a defined framework." She pointed at the picture of the wave that hung before them. "Remember what you told me before I left for India? About living according to a plan that frames one's entire life, and not just based on what's happening right now? Well, I don't yet know what my future holds, but I'm determined to figure it out," Harley said with conviction.

"I don't get it ... what is your plan for the near future?"

"I will get a job at an architecture and design firm and will give it all I've got for a few years. If my heart tells me that this is the work I'm meant to do, then I'll consider getting this graduate degree and dedicate the rest of the Explorer stage to becoming a worthy architect."

Sarah nodded her head in disapproval. "Don't you understand that these kinds of opportunities might never return?" she said, pointing at the envelope with the King's Crown logo. "And what about the scholarship? Have you thought about that part?"

Harley considered telling her mother about Uncle Charlie's check, but held back at the last moment. Even though she had promised her mother she would not hide things from her again, here she was, doing just that. Sarah shot a quizzical look at her daughter, wondering why the conversation had come to a halt. Harley took a quick breath and shifted gears.

"There's one more thing we need to talk about," she said. Her mother raised her eyebrows, as if expecting another major announcement. Her intuition was right on track.

"Mark wants to see you," said Harley. Sarah's face froze. Harley pressed on.

"Mom, I went through the biggest adventure of my life with him. He's a true friend and what happened to Dad is not his fault. Dad brought it on himself. You simply have to forgive Mark."

Her mother was silent for a long moment, then said, "I can't forgive him for what happened. Mark came back in one piece, while we paid a heavy price." Standing up, she went into the kitchen to wash the dishes, leaving her daughter alone and confused.

CHAPTER 19

"CHARLIE WOULD LIKE TO SEE you," Harley informed Shelby over the phone. She was met by silence at the other end of the line.

"He'd really like to see you," she tried again. The silence deepened.

"Mark, maybe this is an opportunity to put it all behind you? He's my uncle, my father's only brother," Harley emphasized.

"All behind me?" Shelby finally said skeptically.

"Don't you think it's time to crack the crust that has formed around everything you kept hidden all these years?" The personal truths the two of them had learned in India had to mean something here at home too. Harley believed this with all her being.

She gave him the address of the steakhouse. "I'll tell Charlie you'll be there next Tuesday evening at seven. Good luck," she said, ending the conversation and wondering if Shelby would accept the invitation. Judging by the phone call, she doubted he and Charlie were going to meet anytime soon.

A week later, getting out of a taxi, Shelby was met with a gust of cold wind. He opened a heavy oak door and entered the dimly lit steakhouse. Above a bar made of polished mahogany was a large mirror. He caught his reflection in it and nervously looked away. The hostess, a young woman in a dress with flowers that accentuated her blue eyes, approached him with a polite smile. "Do you have a reservation?" she asked.

"Yes. I'm meeting Charlie."

Her smile widened. "Certainly. He's waiting for you. May I take your coat?"

Shelby followed her. Charlie was sitting in the corner at a round table, in front of a lit fireplace. When he saw Shelby, he gestured with his drink to the empty chair next to him. Shelby sat down.

"It's been years, Charlie," he said with a slight smile. Charlie smiled back, but his eyes remained cold and expressionless. His lips curved into a thin line as he said, "Years, and not a day has gone by when I didn't wait to hear what had really happened to my brother."

The words were like a punch to Shelby's gut. He took a deep breath, realizing a warm welcome was not in the works. Charlie nodded, as if he understood what Shelby must be experiencing but didn't care one bit.

"Still teaching?"

"Yes," Shelby replied.

Taking a swig of his drink, Charlie said, "Still teaching . . . how wonderful. You should try this Japanese whiskey. Aged eighteen years. Quite a rare find."

"I don't drink anymore." Shelby flagged down the waitress and ordered a seltzer with lemon.

"Any particular reason?"

"Let's just say I don't need it anymore."

Charlie didn't reply, causing Shelby to wonder how much Harley had told him. The fireplace gave off a pleasant heat, but Shelby remained cold and uncomfortable. He waited for Charlie to speak, and after a minute Charlie's eyes rested on him.

"I remember when Jack told me you decided to follow in his footsteps and become a professor."

"That's right," Shelby confirmed. "He was always the trailblazer."

The two men fell silent again. Shelby turned toward a mural depicting a battle between a knight and a dragon. The knight, in shining armor, sat tall atop a noble white horse with a black star on its forehead. The horse was on its hind legs. The knight was holding a long spear that was directed at a crouching dragon spitting purple fire. From the mural, it was hard to say who would win the battle.

"I assume Harley told you the gist of it," Shelby said somberly.

"Yes, that you were the last person to see him alive."

Shelby shrank back at the resentful look on Charlie's face. He spoke in quick sentences: "I tried to dissuade him from climbing the glacier. There was a blizzard that had started a few days before and wouldn't let up. It was impossible to see anything. Jack was determined to make it to the ice cave, no matter what. Finally, I gave in and told him that I would go with him. And I intended to, even though I had no illusions about how dangerous it would be. But in the morning when I woke up—"

"He was already gone," Charlie completed the sentence. "I hope you enjoyed that sleep of yours."

"—It was too late. I searched for him for a few days but couldn't find a trace."

"How reckless," Charlie muttered to himself. Shelby wasn't sure if he was referring to him or to his brother. "How reckless," he repeated.

Shelby saw the pain Charlie felt at the thought of his brother dying in a preventable accident. He noticed the worry lines etched on his face from all the years Charlie had waited to receive even a shred of reliable news. Without thinking, he reached across the table and touched Charlie's shoulder. Charlie flinched as if bitten by a snake.

"I'm sorry I wasn't brave enough to tell you what happened," Shelby said, choking up.

"You could have done more," Charlie said. His eyes glistened. "Maybe you were hoping Jack wouldn't make it back from the glacier so you could be with Sarah and get full credit for that Principle of Eighteen theory Harley told me about."

Shelby's heart pounded. "I never published anything relating to this theory. And as for Sarah . . ." his words trailed off.

"Don't think I forgot that you were madly in love with her," Charlie said, narrowing his eyes. "That's probably why she never told me you were there. She was afraid I'd try to take revenge."

Shelby felt the air around him freeze. He had experienced enough in his life to know when he was being threatened. He looked at Charlie's face, at the eyes that were so similar to Jack's. He realized that despite the resemblance, Charlie was not the man his brother was. He scooted his chair back and stood up. "This conversation is over," he declared with a clenched jaw. "I'm not going to sit here and listen to this pile of accusations and threats."

Unimpressed, Charlie took another sip of his drink.

"You can feed Harley whatever stories you like," Charlie told Shelby. "She's young and looks up to you," he said flatly. "But I believe that if you had been a true friend and done everything in your power to stop my brother, he would be sitting here with me now. You're a liar and a coward, and don't think Sarah doesn't know it. Women have strong intuition about these things."

Shelby stood in place, unable to move. Averting Charlie's gaze, he turned his head toward the mural of the knight fighting the dragon and suddenly remembered the conversation he had had with Harley about the need to slay your own dragons, the ones guarding the treasure in the cave.

"On that fateful day on the glacier, we both lost a brother," Shelby found the strength to speak.

"How dare you say such a thing?" Charlie retorted, slamming his fist on the table and rattling his drink.

"The pain of losing Jack doesn't belong only to you," Shelby continued. "He was like my brother too. He took great ..." Unable to complete his sentence, he turned his gaze to the fireplace. The two men remained quiet for a long time. Finally, Shelby rose from his chair and began walking out.

As he pushed open the door, the hostess called out his name. Shelby turned around and saw her holding his coat. Distractedly, he thanked her. Outside, he didn't feel the cold wind blowing, didn't hear the cars passing by, didn't smell the chestnuts roasting. He walked aimlessly, his thoughts swirling like the falling leaves.

CHAPTER 20

MARK SHELBY WASN'T RETURNING ANY of Harley's calls. When she dialed his office, she was told he was on sick leave and that they didn't know when or if he would be back. After a nerve-racking week he finally called her. He sounded worn out.

"Are you alright?" Harley asked. "I've been trying to reach you."

"Yes, everything's fine," Shelby said, without elaborating.

"Did you meet with Charlie?"

"Yes."

"And?"

"He will never forgive me."

"What happened?"

"I would like to see your mother," Shelby replied, dismissing Harley's question. "There are a few more things I'd like to tell her in person. And perhaps we can finish our work on the Principle of Eighteen, publish the results, and dedicate the book to Jack's memory."

Harley thought this was a lovely idea but doubted her mother would even agree to meet with Shelby, let alone work with him. Keeping these thoughts to herself, she said, "I'll see what I can do."

That night she spoke with her mother at length, explaining how Shelby had saved her life in the blizzard and why Sarah should give him a second chance. Seeing that her daughter was not going to give up, Sarah finally relented, and agreed to the meeting. Harley called Shelby and detected the same hesitation in his voice that he'd displayed when she arranged the meeting with Charlie.

"I don't know, Harley. Maybe we'll wait a little longer," he said.

"You asked for this meeting," she reminded him. "Do you really want to wait another eight years?"

It was quiet at the other end of the line, then Shelby said, "It didn't end well with Charlie. I'm not sure I'm ready for another meeting like that."

Harley nodded. Knowing her uncle, she could only imagine how Charlie had conducted himself. She wondered how to respond. Then, suddenly, she knew exactly what she needed to say.

"Do you remember what the swami told you in the cave? About how to bring joy back into your life?" she asked.

"We're not in a cave in the Himalayas," remarked Shelby.

Harley felt her frustration grow; they were at an impasse. Taking a deep breath, she said, "Mark, you have an opportunity to start a new chapter in your life as well as in my mother's life. Why aren't you embracing it? We may not be in that cave anymore, but I bet the swami is still there, sitting outside with his eyes closed. And I'll bet that if you were there now, he'd still tell you the same thing."

"Let me think about it," Shelby said. "I'll be in touch."

Harley informed her mother that Shelby would be coming for breakfast on Sunday. After waiting all week to hear from him, she decided to show up outside his classroom and wait for him to finish his lecture. When Shelby spotted her in the hallway, he signaled for her to wait. When he approached her, he gave her a hug, and a few students gave them a look of surprise.

"You have to stop doing that," Harley said. "To other people you are my former professor, not the man who tried and failed to save my father's life."

Shelby was taken aback by her bluntness, by how confident she had become.

"Sunday it is?" she asked.

"Fine, Harley. You're just as tenacious as your dad. Sunday it is," he agreed.

"Great. Be there at ten. Expect pancakes. It's the only thing my mother knows how to make." Despite her best efforts, a smile escaped from Harley's lips.

The week passed quickly, and Sunday turned out to be bright and beautiful. The air was clear, almost like in the Indian Himalayas. While she waited for Shelby outside her building, Harley thought about the influence her parents had had on her life. She had inherited her adventurous nature from her father and embraced his unique perspective that life was not something to fear, that it was possible to leap into the unknown from time to time and see where it would lead you. Her father had also left her with the ability to look at life with humor and make spontaneous decisions. At the same time, the way Harley's father saw the world came at a price. His daring nature was accompanied by recklessness and an urge to rebel against prevailing customs.

Her mother saw the world differently. She had self-discipline and believed in hard work instead of shortcuts. Harley knew she took more after her father, but the journey to Gangotri had revealed a thoughtful, even responsible side she hadn't known she possessed.

As she contemplated the parts of her that were entirely her own, an idea started to crystalize in her mind. *What if I took the adventurous side from my father and added a sprinkle of practicality from my mother? Could this unique combination work for me in the years ahead?* Lost in thought, Harley failed to notice Shelby standing in front of her. His hair was neatly brushed, and he was wearing an ironed white shirt and a faded leather jacket. In his hand he held a beautiful bouquet of irises.

"You brought her favorite flowers," Harley said admiringly. Shelby smiled but his eyes were serious. He brushed his hair back with his fingers and loosened his shoulders. Harley thought she had never seen him this tense, not even when she'd first learned of the secret he'd been keeping from her, or when they'd been stuck in the blizzard in the Himalayas.

"She's nervous too," she assured him.

Shelby glanced up and down the street, even though no one was passing by. Then he slowly looked back at Harley.

"What are you planning to do with your life now? Are you still thinking about becoming an architect?" he asked. Harley smiled, suspecting he was stalling before going upstairs. "You're beginning to sound like my mother," she replied. "I'm thinking about working at an architecture and design firm for a few years, to see if architecture is the right fit for me. Don't forget I'm just entering the Explorer stage . . ."

Shelby clasped his hands together, pleased with her answer. "You are on the right track," he said encouragingly.

"You know that I've forgiven you for what happened with my father. You're not to blame for any of it," Harley said with conviction.

Shelby smiled weakly. "I've thought about everything we went through together," he said. "I don't know how I managed to live with myself and my web of lies all these years."

"Mark, you did everything you could. You thought people would assume you didn't do enough. That's why you
never told anyone. But the fact is that my father could
not have been stopped." Harley paused at the painful
truth of her statement. "You have to stop feeling so much
regret. My father was lucky to have a friend like you."

After a grateful hug, Shelby walked to the elevator
and raised two fingers to signal goodbye. Harley headed
toward the park. Foliage swirled around her, stirring up
fragments of memories from the past month. She recalled
Professor Shelby's lecture that had led her to India, the
conversation with Uncle Charlie in his mansion, the first
time she met Rajou, her adventures along the trek, the
swami's cave, and everything she'd learned about her
father and herself.

She had set out to discover what had happened to her
father but ended up achieving even more: She now had
a solid plan for her future and was eager to fulfill the
promise of the Explorer stage. And thanks to her help,
Shelby and her mother might start a new chapter in their
lives. Whatever their future held was now beyond her
control. She had done all she could do, and it was time to
let go. If Rajou were with her now, this is what he would
have told her.

The wind became fiercer. A purple clover-shaped leaf
fell in front of her; she caught and gently held it. When
she looked up, she saw a squirrel on a tall branch, studying her. Eventually it turned its head toward a bigger

branch on the tree next to him. He looked like he was measuring the distance between the two branches, and hesitating. *Leap, you'll be fine*, Harley thought. *You won't fall.*

As if he could read her mind, the squirrel gracefully leapt from one branch to the other, unharmed. Placing the leaf inside her coat pocket, Harley began walking up the street. She passed by a busy restaurant where a young waiter was filling water cups from a pitcher. As she saw a few drops spill to the floor, a memory surfaced of that charmed night on the Ganges River. Rajou had told her about the Kumbh Mela festival, and the legend about the epic fight between gods and demons over a magical pitcher containing an immortality potion, which ended up in a few spilled drops in the Ganges.

She recalled that the next festival would take place in several months, and a quiet joy bubbled inside her. The cold wind tugging at her clothes, Harley raised the collar of her jacket and picked up her pace. As the purple autumn leaves crunched beneath her feet, she kept walking through the chilly wind, her body warm and her heart filled with excited anticipation about her life ahead.

The End

ABOUT THE AUTHOR

EYAL DANON IS THE AUTHOR behind *The Golden Key of Gangotri*. His other books include *Before the Kids and Mortgage*, a humorous travel memoir on backpacking around the world for one year, and *The Principle of 18*, an innovative self-help system for getting the most out of every stage of your life by fulfilling the promise of five distinct life chapters.

Eyal is a Columbia University-trained life coach, and the founder of Ignite Advisory Group, a global leader in creating expert communities. He lives in New Jersey with his family, trying to embrace the four seasons of the Northeast after growing up surfing the Mediterranean Sea. He enjoys reading anything by J.R.R. Tolkien, hiking, table tennis, and Japanese whiskey.

Connect with Eyal at eyaldanon.com

CPSIA information can be obtained
at www.ICGtesting.com
Printed in the USA
JSHW030006100721
16783JS00001B/2